BARCELONA

Dan Colwell

JPM Publications

Contents

- This Way Barcelona — 3
- Flashback — 5
- Sightseeing — 13
- La Rambla — 14
- Ciutat Vella — 17
- El Raval — 29
- Waterfront — 33
- Montjuïc — 35
- Eixample and Gracìa — 41
- Around Barcelona — 49
- Excursions — 51
- Dining Out — 58
- Entertainment — 66
- The Hard Facts — 72
- Index — 79

Maps
- Costa Brava — 52
- Costa Daurada — 55
- Barcelona, town centre and metro (fold-out)

▌*Page 1: Columbus at the waterfront*

This Way Barcelona

Buzzing Barcelona
Within minutes of your first walk along La Rambla you'll realise that you're in one of the most exciting cities in the world. This long street running through the old town simply fizzes with energy. The flow of people is so great, and there's so much going on, that it feels like Carnival every day of the year. And yet far from being an exception, La Rambla sets the tone for all of Barcelona.

The city has plenty to be excited about. Its dynamism and diversity extend from an ebullient café culture and exuberant nightlife to ultra-modern centres of contemporary art and cutting-edge urban developments. There are world-class museums devoted to Picasso and Miró, and in the Barri Gòtic the city has the most well-preserved medieval quarter in Europe. It is also home to the extraordinary architecture of Antoni Gaudí, the presiding genius of Modernisme, the home-grown version of Art Nouveau. Barceloneses can ruminate on all this at any number of restaurants, where they will be served first-rate Catalonian cuisine with its own proud tradition separate from the rest of Spain. And when they want to get away from the bustle of the city, they could be lying on a beach, skiing in the mountains or sampling wines at vineyards in rolling countryside all within a few hours of the centre.

Canny Catalonians
This vibrant metropolis of 1.5 million people has long enjoyed a reputation in Spain for its business acumen and industriousness, and the citizens pride themselves on their *seny*, the Catalan word for a solid, commonsense approach to life. For centuries Barcelona has been the economic powerhouse of the country. It's the birthplace of Spain's industrial revolution, the foremost port in the Mediterranean, and the commercial focus of the country's connection to the rest of Europe. But it's not just because of this that Barceloneses look away from Madrid and see themselves as more like their northern counterparts in Paris or London. For apart from being undoubtedly cosmopolitan, they also think of their city as a national capital. Until the end of the 15th century, Barcelona was at the centre of an independent Catalan state, which had its own laws

and language, and even ran a Mediterranean empire. Although the empire was lost, its collective *seny* remained intact and the city continued to prosper. Thankfully, though, Catalonian common sense sometimes goes magnificently awry, and it is the moments of wild extravagance that we can thank for such extraordinary monuments as the fairytale Parc Güell, the surreal Magic Fountain near Plaça Espanya, and the city waterfront, renovated for the 1992 Olympic Games.

The people's love affair with their city is all too evident. Over the centuries they have created an abundance of viewpoints from which to admire it. Try the Columbus Monument for a superb vista of the revamped old port. Or in the centre of the Gothic Quarter, find your way up to the top of King Martin's 16th-century lookout tower, from where Barcelona's medieval world of high-altitude gargoyles, terracotta rooftops and hidden courtyards is magically revealed. The 19th-century expansion of the city known as the Eixample provides a remarkable highpoint—the otherworldly spire of the Sagrada Família church is guaranteed to give you an unforgettable perspective on Barcelona. The lucky Barceloneses have, of course, been helped along by Mother Nature, who did her bit by providing some perfectly placed hills around the edge of town. Since 1992, the loftiest panorama has been from the Collserola tower on top of Mount Tibidabo. Here, the whole of Barcelona is laid out spectacularly before you.

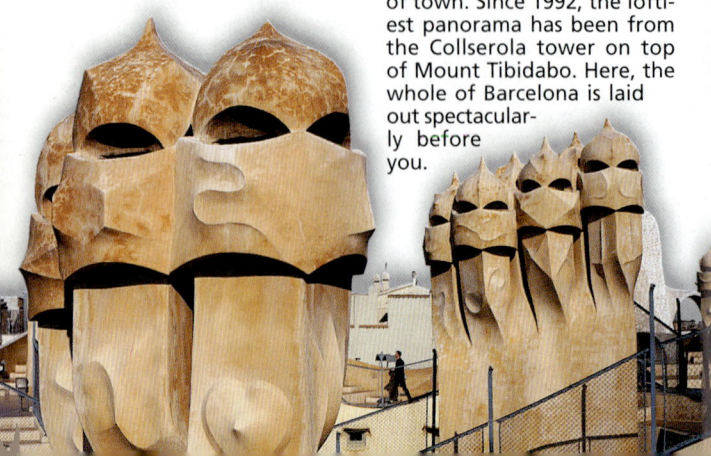

Flashback

Early History

Legend has it that Barcelona was founded by the Carthaginians, who had settlements along Spain's Mediterranean coast, and that it was named after their leader Hamil Barca, father of Hannibal. In fact, the earliest-known settlers in the region were the *Laietani*, a Bronze Age Celt-Iberian tribe who specialized in producing grain and harvesting oysters, and there was no town established here until the Romans turned up some time in the 1st century BC. Their main centre was at Tarragona, to the south, and at first Barcelona was just a military camp. It became an official colony around 15 BC under the Emperor Augustus, and given the name Faventia Julia Augusta Pia Barcino.

The town remained a minor, albeit prosperous outpost for 200 years, known mainly for its manufacture of wine, olive oil and garum, a fermented anchovy sauce that was exported throughout the empire. It had a Jewish community in place by the 2nd century AD, and around the year 300 acquired its first patron saint, the Christian martyr Santa Eulàlia. But the secure life of a Mediterranean colony was under threat. The empire was facing invasion from northern barbarians and the city walls had to be strengthened with huge stone blocks during the 4th century, many of which are still visible today.

Of Visigoths, Moors and Franks

From 409, successive waves of Vandal, Alani and Suevian tribes swept over the Pyrenees and invaded Spain. Each one ransacked Barcelona and then headed south, so when the Visigoths entered the city in 415 under King Ataulf and made it the centre of their new kingdom, the inhabitants were at least promised some stability. Indeed, the Visigoth occupation was to last three centuries and eventually extended to almost the whole of Spain. The new rulers turned out to be great believers in jurisprudence, embellishers of churches and altogether most un-barbarian in character. A series of baronies evolved under the central authority of the king, but by the 8th century the system was disintegrating, with the king and his barons in perpetual conflict.

Such political disunity was an open invitation to the next

invader eyeing up Spain's rich lands, though this time the danger lay to the south. In 711, Arab armies crossed the Straits of Gibraltar from Africa and overwhelmed the Visigoths. They reached Barcelona six years later and continued on into southern France, where they stayed until defeated by the Franks under Charlemagne at the end of the 8th century. The Franks pushed the Moors back across the Pyrenees, and in 801 Barcelona was liberated by Charlemagne's son, Louis the Pious. It then became part of Louis's *Marca Hispanica* (Spanish March), a buffer zone between Moorish Spain and the Frankish empire that occupies roughly the area of modern Catalonia. Given that the Moors would stay in Spain for nearly seven more centuries, Catalonia's cultural and linguistic separateness from the rest of the country, and its fierce sense of independence, can be dated from this time.

The Franks left the region under the command of a number of counts, who guarded the border and fought off Moorish incursions. One of them was the Count of Barcelona, Guifré el Pilós (Wilfred the Hairy), a man famous not just for the abundance of his body hair, but also for establishing something approaching a Catalonian state towards the end of the 9th century. He did it by conquering the various counties of the Spanish March and uniting them under his rule, which afterwards became hereditary. Catalonia was still nominally in the Frankish domain. But when the Moors raided Barcelona in 985, and the request for aid from the Franks was ignored, Wilfred's great-grandson, Borrell II, used the occasion to declare Catalonian independence.

Medieval Golden Age

Barcelona entered the new millennium in upbeat mood. Either by marriage or purchase, successive counts had set about acquiring more territory. The city's economy was starting to boom, and a code of law known as the *Usatges*, an early sort of *Magna Carta*, had been instituted by Ramon Berenguer I in 1064–68 guaranteeing citizens' rights. Things were shaping up nicely for a Catalan Golden Age.

It began in earnest in 1137, when Count Ramon Berenguer IV married Petronella, heiress to the throne of Catalonia's neighbouring state of Aragon, and received the whole king-

A splash of colourful turn-of-the-century taste in the medieval Barri Gòtic.

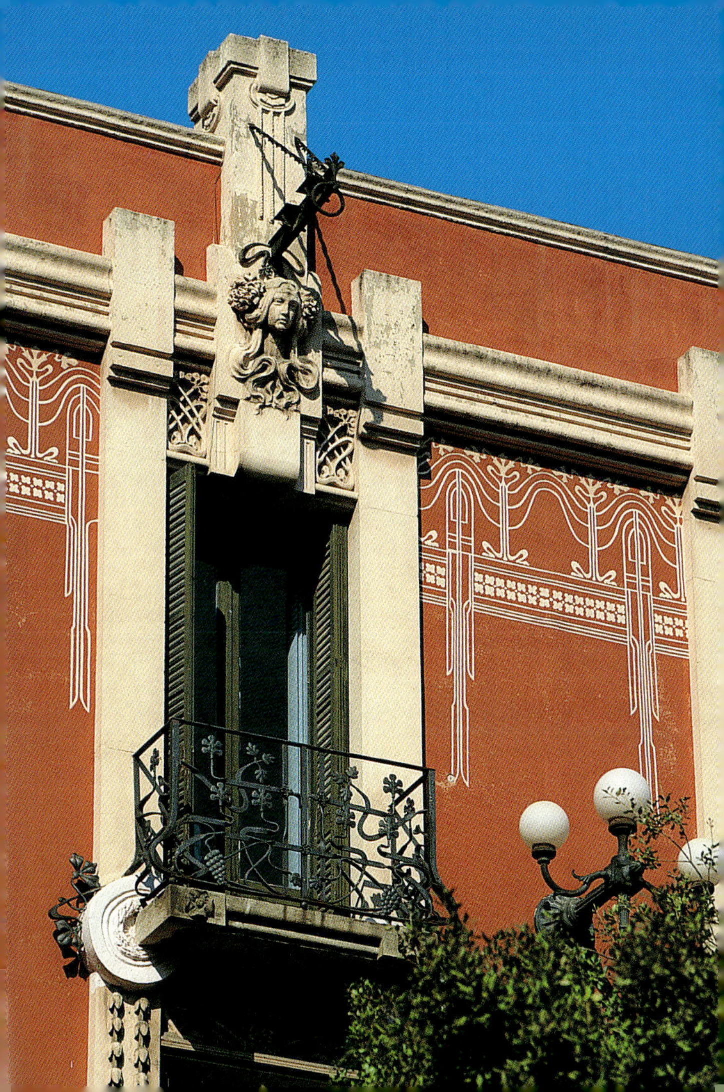

dom as a dowry. With the new title of Count-King (*comte-reis*), and a greatly increased military and financial capability, Barcelona's rulers began to harbour dreams of empire, and looked out to the Mediterranean as the place where they would be realised.

Under Jaume I (1213–76) and his immediate descendants through to the middle of the 14th century, Catalonia conquered the Balearic Islands, Sardinia, Sicily and established trading posts as far as Athens, Constantinople and Beirut. Catalonian merchants flourished, and the wealth they created flowed back into the city, funding the construction of Barcelona's Barri Gòtic, with its magnificent Gothic cathedral, churches and mansions. Meanwhile, Catalan became established as a literary language, with translations of the Bible and the Classics, Jaume I's autobiographical *Book of Deeds* about his military exploits, and other works of philosophy and poetry being written in it.

Catalonia Falls, Spain Rises

Even as Barcelona reached its peak of achievement in the reign of Pere III (1336–87), when the Saló del Tinell, the Drassanes shipyard and much of the cathedral were built, things were already beginning to fall apart. In 1348 the city was devastated by the Black Death, which reached it via the colony of Majorca. In the wake of the plague came famine and epidemics, and in 1391 a terrible pogrom was carried out against the Jews, who were blamed for the disasters.

The unbroken line of Counts of Barcelona stretching back to Wilfred the Hairy ended with the death of Martí I in 1410, and the throne passed to Ferdinand of Antequera. From now on, Catalonia would be ruled by Castilians. As the 15th century progressed, the great days of Catalan power slowly trickled away. Mercantile rivals such as the Genoese and the Venetians began to dominate Mediterranean trade. In 1462 a 10-year civil war broke out between the monarchy and the Catalan upper classes. Soon after it had ended, the new king, Ferdinand II, married the future Isabella I of Castile, and Spain was united as a single nation.

The main effect was to shift political power from Barcelona to Madrid, something that was compounded by Christopher Columbus's discovery of the Americas in 1492, after which Spain's gaze was fixed firmly westwards away from the Mediterranean. Worse still,

Flashback

Halfway down La Rambla at Plaça de la Boqueria, the circular mosaic is by Joan Miró.

Catalans were barred from trading with the New World colonies. Madrid became the official capital of the empire in 1561 under the Habsburg king of Spain, Philip II, while Catalonia suffered the indignity of having a Habsburg viceroy imposed upon it.

Disaffection mounted, and in 1640 a popular uprising by peasants (known as the War of the Reapers) saw Catalonia declare its independence from Spain. Twelve years of war left the region exhausted and back under the control of Madrid. Then, during the War of Spanish Succession that followed the end of the Habsburg line in 1700, Catalonia sided with the English, Dutch and Germans against the Bourbon candidate, Philip V. When their allies signed the Treaty of Utrecht leaving Philip V on the throne, the Catalans had to face the consequences, and Barcelona was besieged by Spanish troops once again. This time, a huge fort, the Ciutadella, was built to keep an eye on the unruly Catalans, their ancient city government was dismantled, and the use of the Catalan language in writing and education was banned.

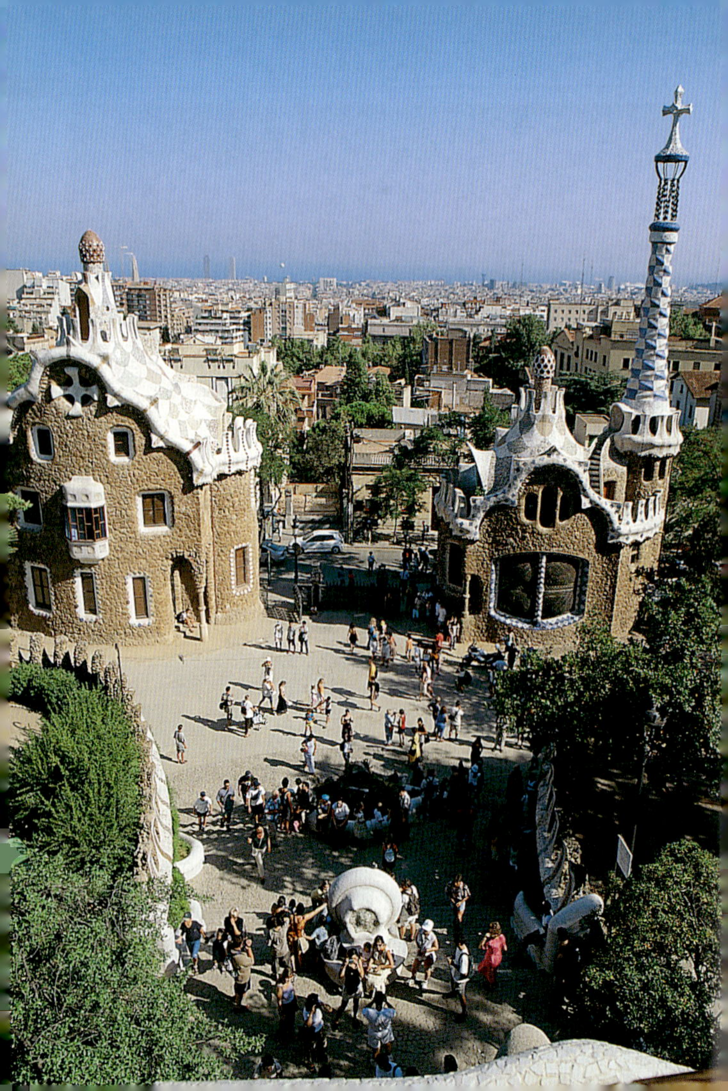

The Catalan Renaissance

Oddly enough, one result of Catalonia's fuller absorption into the Spanish state was a turnaround in its economic position. This was mainly due to the development of the cotton industry and, from 1778, the lifting of the ban on trade with the Americas. There was a temporary setback when Barcelona was caught up in the turmoil of the Napoleonic Wars and occupied by French troops, but by the middle of the 19th century the city had regained its confidence, which had risen to a level not seen since the Middle Ages.

Like then, this was manifested in two important fields, architecture and the Catalan language. New works of literature in Catalan were published and the Institute of Catalan Studies was set up in 1906. But Barcelona's cultural dynamism was most evident in the remarkable buildings that went up at the end of the 19th century. The huge extension of the city beyond the old town—the Eixample—began in 1860, and over the following decades its great boulevards became home to some of Barcelona's most radical Modernista (Art Nouveau) architecture, commissioned by the wealthy middle classes and designed by leading Catalan architects such as Antoni Gaudí and Lluís Domènech i Montaner. The focal point of this *Renaixença* (Renaissance), as the period came to be called, was the 1888 Universal Exposition. It proved to be a dazzling showcase for Barcelona's industrial and cultural talent, and attracted one and a half million visitors—and yet, with the splendid array of new building projects it engendered, it almost bankrupted the city.

Civil War and General Franco

Alongside the prosperity, however, there grew a dissatisfied class of poor workers. Anarchist and republican groups developed with the aim of challenging the established order, and with an influx of immigrants from other parts of Spain adding to the mix, the early 20th century saw increasing social and political upheaval. This culminated in the *Setmana Tràgica*, or Tragic Week in 1909, when workers rioted against conscription for a colonial war in Morocco and set fire to churches. In retaliation, they were shot down by

The two pavilions at the entrance to Parc Güell look like something out of a fairy tale.

troops, and later their leaders were rounded up and five of them executed.

A strong Catalan separatist movement developed around this time as well, and on the back of its industrial success the region was able to regain some of the political autonomy lost in the 18th century. With Spain a non-combatant, Barcelona did well out of World War I by supplying arms and equipment to the French. Its continuing role as the nation's economic powerhouse was demonstrated once more in the 1929 International Exhibition, in preparation for which the Montjuïc and Plaça d'Espanya areas were given extensive overhauls.

Things turned dramatically for the worse in the 1930s, however, when Spain's newly elected Republican government was overthrown by right-wing forces under General Franco. The city lived up to its longstanding radical tradition and proved the main centre of resistance against Franco, but was defeated in January 1939. As with Philip V two centuries earlier, reprisals took the form of withdrawal of Catalan political and linguistic rights. The city now entered its grey period, with 20 years of economic and cultural depression.

Barcelona Today

Barcelona was bouncing back even before the death of General Franco in 1975, benefiting financially from the new industry of mass tourism on the nearby Costa Brava. Within two years of the end of Franco's rule, democratic elections were held and Catalonia regained its regional political authority, the Generalitat, under a Catalan president, Jordi Pujol. Barcelona soon re-established itself as the most fast-paced, industrious and above all stylish city in Spain. Education, literature and even the street signs were now in Catalan. And Barcelona once again used the occasion of a major event—this time the 1992 Olympics—to transform itself. In particular, the old, disused waterfront received a facelift and gave the city a fine new leisure area. Most Catalans now seem to accept that their state will not become independent from the rest of Spain; but with Barcelona firmly established as one of Europe's greatest cities, an inspiration for architects and planners from across the continent and a magnet for visitors from around the world, they have entered the new millennium with as much confidence in their culture as they did the last one.

Sightseeing

The historic centre of Barcelona is the Ciutat Vella (Old Town), the site of the original Roman settlement and later the basis of the Barri Gòtic, or medieval quarter. The rest of the city is easily reached from here, either on foot or by public transport.

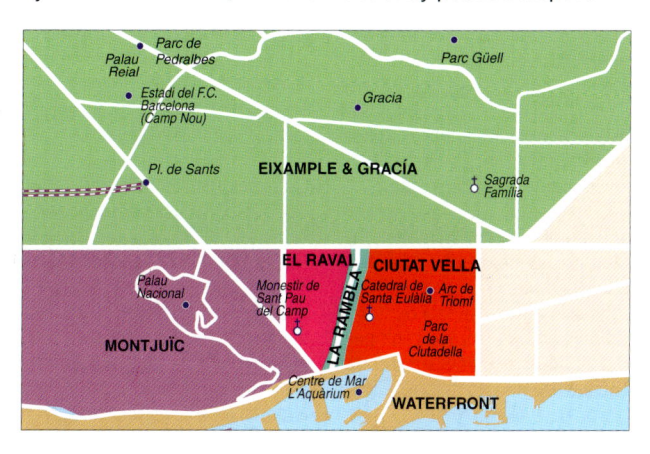

14 **La Rambla**: Barcelona's vibrant main thoroughfare through the centre of town down to the waterfront

17 **Ciutat Vella**: around the cathedral, the ancient core of the modern city

29 **El Raval**: colourful area of narrow streets and old bars

33 **Waterfront**: beaches, and the bustling revamped Port Vell and Port Olímpic

35 **Montjuïc**: superb museums on a hill overlooking the city

41 **Eixample & Gràcia**: Modernista buildings galore in the 19th-century extension of Barcelona, northwards into the hills

Sightseeing

LA RAMBLA

Enthralling and dramatic, La Rambla is one of the world's most spectacular shows, with a performance that goes on almost every minute of the day and night, and a cast made up of the thousands of people who continually pass up and down along the swirling patterns of its black-and-white paving stones. To add to the fun, it's packed with news-stands, birdsellers, palm-readers, three-card tricksters, buskers and street-performers. In fact, this glorious 2-kilometre, tree-lined boulevard has so much for the eye to take in that it can feel ten times as long, and yet still you can't help but agree with the Spanish poet Lorca when he said that he wished it would never end.

La Rambla W 1–Y 6*
- Metro: Catalunya/Liceu/
- Drassanes

La Rambla first took on its modern appearance in the 18th century, and the slightly meandering shape of the street is due to the fact that it was laid over a dry riverbed along whose banks the western wall of the medieval Barri Gòtic had been built (the name comes from the Arabic word *ramla*, meaning "riverbed"). It runs from the vast Plaça de Catalunya down to the Columbus statue and the port, and strictly speaking changes its name five times along the way, with each part of the boulevard recording the names of churches or convents it once passed. Look at the street signs as you go and you'll see you're actually on Rambla de Canaletes, Rambla Estudis, Rambla Sant Josep, Rambla Caputxins and Rambla Santa Monica.

The best thing to do on La Rambla is simply join the stream of people and enjoy the unrivalled pleasure of the *paseo* here. But there are a few notable sights en route that are worth pausing over—and don't forget to look up as you stroll along, at the fascinating upper storeys of the buildings.

At the top end, the **Font de Canaletes** is a drinking fountain, a taste of whose water is said to guarantee a return trip to Barcelona. A little further down on the right, the roof of the **Teatre Poliorama** is where George Orwell spent a few days during the Spanish Civil War training his rifle on the Civil Guards holed up at the Café Moka opposite. Just before you reach the Mercat de la

---

*References correspond to the fold-out map at the end of the guide.

La Ramba

Boqueria, be sure to take in the fine neoclassical façade of the **Palau de la Virreina** at La Rambla 99. It was built in the 1770s by a returning viceroy of Peru, and is one of the first signs in Barcelona of the new wealth created by the trade with Spain's American colonies. A short distance after the market there's a large pavement **mosaic** in the middle of La Rambla designed by Joan Miró in 1976. To the left, where the roads from the Barri Gòtic converge, the extraordinary **Casa Bruno Quadras** building has an intriguing green Chinese dragon acting as a lamp holder.

Mercat de la Boqueria X 4
- Metro: Liceu
- La Rambla 91
- Tel. 93 318 25 84
- Mon–Sat 8 a.m.–8.30 p.m.

Barcelona's most important food market was built in the 19th century. Beneath its vast network of wrought-iron vaulting is one of the great sights of the city, a truly mouth-watering display of fresh fruit and nuts, spices and herbs, and mounds of fish, sausages, meat and cheeses.

You never know who you're going to come across on the Ramblas.

Sightseeing

Museu de l'Eròtica X 4
- Metro: Liceu
- La Rambla 96
- Tel. 93 318 98 65
- Open daily 10 a.m.–10 p.m.

On the other side of La Rambla from the market, this attempt to give a serious historical perspective on the subject of all things erotic is not entirely convincing. But that doesn't mean some of its displays, such as the collection of photos depicting Barcelona's racy Barrio Chino district in the 1930s, are anything less than fascinating.

Plaça Reial X 4
- Metro: Liceu

Just off La Rambla, and reached by the narrow C/de Colom, the Plaça Reial is an impressive 19th-century square of handsome neoclassical façades. The two lampposts in the centre are the earliest known work of the great Modernista architect, Antoni Gaudí. The palm-shaded square, built on the site of a Capuchin convent, attracts an odd social mix, which it just about manages to balance harmoniously—its colonnades harbour several bars and a couple of Barcelona's trendiest restaurants, yet for some time it has also had a well-earned reputation for being the hangout of the city's down-and-outs.

Museu de Cera Y 5
- Metro: Drassanes
- Passatge de la Banca 7
- Tel. 93 317 26 49
- Mid July–mid Sept daily 10 a.m.–10 p.m.;
- mid Sept–mid July Mon–Fri 10 a.m.–1.30 p.m., 4–7.30 p.m.;
- Sat, Sun 11 a.m.–2 p.m., 4.30–8.30 p.m.

A small passage leads to the Wax Museum, with lots of waxwork tableaux, a chamber of horrors, and models of well-known figures, including some you're unlikely to see in Madame Tussaud's such as General Franco.

Monument a Colom Y 6
- Metro: Drassanes
- Plaça Portal de la Pau
- Tel. 93 302 52 24
- Open daily 10 a.m.–6.30 p.m.

This tall column was built for the Universal Exposition of 1888 and is Barcelona's homage to Christopher Columbus ("Colom" in Catalan). His discovery of America spelt the end of Catalonia's economic independence from Castile, but Columbus was still a hero in Barcelona because the locals fancied that the great explorer was born in their city (he wasn't). You can take a lift to the top for fine views of the recently spruced up port area.

Ciutat Vella

CIUTAT VELLA

The historic old town lies immediately east of La Rambla. The first Roman settlers had their main temple and forum on what is now Plaça Sant Jaume, which has remained the centre of civic life in Catalonia to this day. Most of the architectural treasures of the Barri Gòtic (Gothic Quarter) date from the medieval era, however, and include the magnificent cathedral, royal palace and an atmospheric tangle of narrow streets. Beyond here is the huge Ciutadella park, with a number of fine museums, and Barcelona's no. 1 crowd-puller, the Museu Picasso.

Santa Maria del Pi X 4
- Metro: Liceu
- Plaça Sant Josep Oriol
- Tel. 93 318 47 43
- Mon–Fri 8.30 a.m.–1 p.m., 4.30–8.30 p.m.;
- Sat 8.30 a.m.–1 p.m., 4–9 p.m.;
- Sun 9 a.m.–2 p.m., 5–9 p.m.

If you enter the Ciutat Vella from La Rambla at Plaça Boqueria, you will soon arrive at this classic example of Catalan Gothic architecture. It was begun in 1322, though the octagonal bell tower was added in the following century. The dark, almost austere interior, with its superb single-span nave, is typically Catalan, and the splendid rose window over the entrance is by far the most flamboyant gesture. There are three pleasant little squares around the church, which are popular places to relax at an outside café and enjoy the calm. On the first weekend of every month the area is taken over by an artisan **food and craft market**.

Caelum X 3
- Metro: Liceu
- Bus: all routes to Plaça de Catalunya
- C/ de la Palla 8
- Tel. 93 302 69 93
- Mon–Sat 10.30 a.m.–8.30 p.m.

Over 30 monastery kitchens and convents supply food to this unusual store behind the Palau Episcopal: cheeses, olives, preserves and so on. Tastings are held in the basement, ancient thermal baths converted into a tea room.

Catedral La Seu Y 3
- Metro: Liceu/Jaume I
- Plaça de la Seu
- Tel. 93 315 15 54
- Mon–Fri 8 a.m.–1.30 p.m., 4–7.30 p.m.;
- Sat, Sun 8 a.m.–1.30 p.m., 5–7.30 p.m.
- Museum open daily 10 a.m.–1 p.m.

Sightseeing

Barcelona's spectacular Gothic cathedral is built on a site first occupied by a Roman temple, and later a mosque. The earliest parts of the cathedral date from 1298, and work continued through to the 1440s—though a shortage of cash meant that the façade had to wait until 1890 to be completed, in what some purists consider an overly ornate Gothic Revival style. Inside, elegant, slender pillars soar upwards, marking off the nave from its two aisles, which boast an array of 29 side chapels. The centre of the cathedral is dominated by the *coro*, a characteristically Spanish feature where the carved choir stalls are enclosed within a box-like structure. Between this and the altar, steps lead down to the crypt containing the tomb of Barcelona's patron saint, Eulàlia.

Possibly the most beautiful part of the cathedral is the medieval cloister. Here, among the Gothic arches, ancient tombstones and tall palm trees, you'll also find a gaggle of geese. This eccentric touch goes back centuries—one explanation is

LA SARDANA

The energetic yet graceful national dance of Catalonia, the sardana, with its haunting woodwind accompaniment, hypnotizes Catalans wherever they may be. The exact origins of this disciplined ring dance are unknown. Researchers suggest that Greeks may have introduced it to Catalonia when they were established in Empúrias and elsewhere on the coast.

The deceptively simple-looking sardana is danced in normal everyday clothes, except on special occasions. The dancers form a circle, which grows as newcomers join it. If it proves unwieldy, they just form another. If they run out of space, they make circles within circles. Each group has a leader who keeps meticulous time and signals changes. If he makes one error his ring loses its rhythm and can't complete the final step in time with the band.

The wonder of the sardana is the spirit it generates. The dance cuts all barriers. Doctors and farmers dance together; long-haired students join the same circle as middle-aged housewives. The sardana reminds them that, whatever their social differences, they are Catalans. Even tourists can, technically, join in. In actual fact, prudence is advisable. There is a fairly strict rule that puts an end to most tourists' ambitions: no Catalan would ever move into a circle that has a much higher standard of dancing than he is capable of, and the uninitiated visitor might thus find himself edged out.

In Barcelona, the sardana is danced in front of the cathedral from July to September, Saturday 6 p.m.; Sundays at noon.

Ciutat Vella

It looks Gothic—but the façade of the cathedral was not undertaken until the late 19th century.

that the whiteness of their plumage was intended to evoke the purity of Saint Eulàlia. The Chapter House has a small museum of art, with paintings by Renaissance Catalan artists such as Jaime Huguet and Bartolomé Bermejo. The cloister gives access to the Romanesque Capella de Santa Llúcia, predating the rest of the cathedral.

Leaving the Santa Llúcia chapel by its door onto the street outside, you will find yourself opposite the former archdeacon's house. Dating from the 16th century, it has an exquisite cloister-courtyard with a small fountain and 100-year-old palm tree, as well as views of the Roman gate into which it was built.

Casa de l'Ardiaca Y 3
- Metro: Liceu/Jaume I
- C/de Santa Llúcia
- Tel. 93 318 11 95
- Mon–Fri 9 a.m.–8.30;
- Sat 9 a.m.–1 p.m.

Museu Diocesà Y 2
- Metro: Jaume I
- Avda de la Catedral
- Tel. 93 315 22 13
- Tues–Sat 10 a.m.–2 p.m. and
- 5–8 p.m., Sun 11 a.m.–2 p.m.

Head back to Plaça de la Seu, where this museum is located in the Casa de la Pia Almoina, a 15th-century almshouse that incorporates part of a Roman tower. On display are works of mainly Gothic-era religious art, including paintings, sculptures and altar pieces.

Museu Frederic Marès Y 3
- Metro: Jaume I
- Plaça Sant Iu 5–6
- Tel. 93 310 58 00
- Tues, Thurs 10 a.m.–5 p.m.;
- Wed, Fri, Sat 10 a.m.–7 p.m.;
- Sun 10 a.m.–2 p.m.

Follow the narrow C/dels Comtes to one of Barcelona's more unusual museums. Frederic Marès (1893–1991) was a sculptor, art teacher and obsessive collector of anything and everything that came his way. The display truly ranges from the sublime to the ridiculous—there's a vast quantity of religious sculptures, especially crucifixions and statues of the Virgin, alongside displays of such fripperies as ashtrays, cigarette cards, nutcrackers and perfume flasks. This vast store of objects was given by Marès to the city, and is now housed in a wing of the Palau Reial.

ROAMING WITH THE ROMANS

You can take in most of the remains of the ancient city of Barcino, as the Romans called Barcelona, during a very enjoyable stroll around the labyrinthine streets of the Barri Gòtic. Start on Plaça Nova, near the cathedral. At the start of C/del Bisbe are two massive towers that guarded the entrance to the Roman town. The street leads south to Plaça Sant Jaume, on the site of the Roman forum where the markets were held. You can reach the Temple of Augustus (1st century AD) from C/Paradís on the north side of the square. Go back across Plaça Sant Jaume to C/de la Ciutat, next to the Ajuntament, and follow it to where it runs into C/Regomir. Here, at no. 3, the foundations of some Roman baths can be seen beneath a fine medieval house. Just beyond, turn left onto C/Correu Vell, one of the most attractive streets in the old town. Follow it to the end and you'll see a substantial chunk of one of the original defensive towers. C/del Sots-Tinent Navarro runs northwards near here and continues up to the Palau Reial. This street traces the outer wall of the Roman city, and there are some impressive stretches of the wall still in place, including a considerable part incorporated into the palace itself, best seen from Plaça Berenguer el Gran. This area of Roman Barcelona is revealed in fascinating detail below street level from inside the Museu d'Història de la Ciutat.

Ciutat Vella

Palau Reial Y 3
- Metro: Jaume I
- Plaça del Rei
- Tel. 93 315 11 11
- June–Sept Tues–Sat 10 a.m.–8 p.m.; Sun 10 a.m.–2 p.m.
- Oct–May Tues–Sat 10 a.m.–2 p.m., 4–8 p.m.; Sun 10 a.m.–2 p.m.

Turn left off C/dels Comtes to the well-preserved medieval Plaça del Rei, once the courtyard of the Palau Reial, the royal palace of the Count-Kings of Barcelona.
In the north corner, steps lead up to the magnificent 14th-century **Saló del Tinell**, with its remarkable barrel-like vault and arches that span 17 m. Historians are undecided as to whether it was in here or on the steps outside that Ferdinand and Isabella received Columbus after his return from the Americas. The hall was later used by the Spanish Inquisition as an imposing place of interrogation. Nowadays it holds temporary art exhibitions.
The adjacent **Capella de Santa Agata** was built under Jaume II at the beginning of the 14th century as the palace chapel.
From here, you can climb the 5-storey **Mirador del Rei Martí** (King Martin's watchtower) that overlooks the Plaça del Rei, and enjoy marvellous close-up views of the cathedral and a fine panorama of the city.

Museu d'Història de la Ciutat Y 3
- Metro: Jaume I
- Plaça del Rei
- Tel. 93 315 11 11
- June–Sept Tues–Sat 10 a.m.–8 p.m.; Sun 10 a.m.–2 p.m.
- Oct–May Tues–Sat 10 a.m.–2 p.m., 4–8 p.m.;
- Sun 10 a.m.–2 p.m.

This excellent museum is located at the south end of the square and entered via the Casa Padellàs, a 15th-century mansion that was moved here from nearby C/de Mercaders in 1931. During the work the foundations of a substantial part of the original Roman city were discovered, and these now form the most fascinating part of the museum. Descend by lift to a series of boardwalks that extend beneath Plaça del Rei as far as the cathedral. These take you over ancient roads, houses, shops and factories for making wine, salted fish and garum, a fish sauce highly regarded by the Romans. Upstairs, you'll find exhibitions on the history of the city, including a "virtual history" tour through time, and access to the sumptuous buildings of the Palau Reial.

Sightseeing

Palau de la Generalitat Y 3

- Metro: Jaume I
- Plaça Sant Jaume
- Tel. 93 402 46 00
- Open for guided tours on the 2nd and 4th Sun of each month, 10.30 a.m.–1.30 p.m.

Plaça Sant Jaume is the epicentre of Barcelona's political life. The Generalitat—the Catalan regional government—has been on the north side of the square since the 15th century. The façade is a late-Renaissance addition—but the original Gothic entrance, with a fine sculpture of St George dating from 1418, is by master Catalan architect Marc Safont. It can be seen on C/del Bisbe just around the corner. Access to the building is limited. If you are able to get in, though, you'll find a beautiful medieval cloister and Safont's magnificent chapel of Sant Jordi (St George, Catalonia's patron saint).

Temple d'Augustus Y 3

- Metro: Jaume I
- C/Paradís 10
- Tel. 93 315 11 11
- June–Sept Tues–Sat 10 a.m.–8 p.m.; Sun 10 a.m.–2 p.m. Oct–May Tues–Sat 10 a.m.–2 p.m., 4–8 p.m.; Sun 10 a.m.–2 p.m.

Roman Barcelona's main temple was located just behind Plaça Sant Jaume. It was dedicated to the emperor Caesar Augustus in the 1st century AD. Its four remaining Corinthian columns are hidden away inside an otherwise unassuming building.

Ajuntament de Barcelona Y 3

- Metro: Jaume I
- Plaça Sant Jaume
- Tel. 93 402 70 00
- Sat, Sun 10 a.m.–2 p.m.

Facing the Generalitat across Plaça Sant Jaume—often more in the spirit of rival than colleague—the Ajuntament is Barcelona's City Hall. It has a fairly bland 19th-century neoclassical façade, but like the Generalitat there's an original Gothic one tucked away on a side street, in this case C/de la Ciutat. Much of the splendid 14th-century interior is open to the public at the weekend. Reached by a grand staircase, the highlight of the building is the Saló de Cent. This splendid Catalan-Gothic hall dates from 1369, and gets its name from being the place where the Consell de Cent, a government body consisting of 100 representitive citizens from all classes, regulated city affairs from the mid 13th century to the early 1700s. In the courtyard downstairs, look out for sculptures by Joan Miró and Frederic Marès.

Ciutat Vella

Sants Just i Pastor Y 3
- Metro: Jaume I
- Plaça Sant Just 1
- Tel. 93 301 74 33
- Mon–Sat 9 a.m.–12.45 p.m., 5–8 p.m.; Sun 9 a.m.–1 p.m.

From C/de la Ciutat turn left onto C/Hércules, which leads to this 14th-century Catalan Gothic church with baroque additions. It's on a delightful little square that's a haven of peace in this part of town and a good spot for an inner-city picnic. The Gothic fountain here was built in 1367. A **medieval market** is held on the square on the first Thursday of every month.

La Mercé Y–Z 5
- Metro: Jaume I

C/de la Ciutat leads eventually to C/de la Mercè, just back from the waterfront. This area is noticeably more run down than the northern Barri Gòtic; although it was once one of the most fashionable parts of the city, by the early 20th century it had fallen on hard times. This was when the Picasso family lived here—Picasso Senior taught art at the *Escola de Belles Artes* located in the huge La Llotja building on Passeig Isabel II, while the fledgling artist learnt about life in the tough streets of the district and the brothels of C/d'Avinyó. His first

THE TRAGIC CALL Y 3

Immediately west of Plaça Sant Jaume is the Call, the former Jewish area of Barcelona. The first Jews settled here in the 2nd century AD—which means that they were in Barcelona long before there were any Christians here. By the Middle Ages they were the backbone of the city's flourishing financial and mercantile community and underpinned the burgeoning Mediterranean empire of the Count-Kings. That didn't prevent their victimization by the authorities. Jews had to pay heavy taxes, while a strict curfew meant they had to spend the hours of darkness inside the Call. During the 13th century, under Jaume I, they were forced to wear a red and yellow button on their clothes so they could be easily identified. If this sounds all-too familiar, worse was to follow. Blamed by the populace for the recent plague, a terrible pogrom was carried out in August 1391 and the community massacred. By the time Jews were officially banned from the city in 1424, the Call was already deserted. Walk the tiny side streets of the district around Carrer del Call and Carrer de Ramon del Call and you could fancy yourself back in medieval Barcelona—except that the traces of the community which gave so much to the city have virtually disappeared.

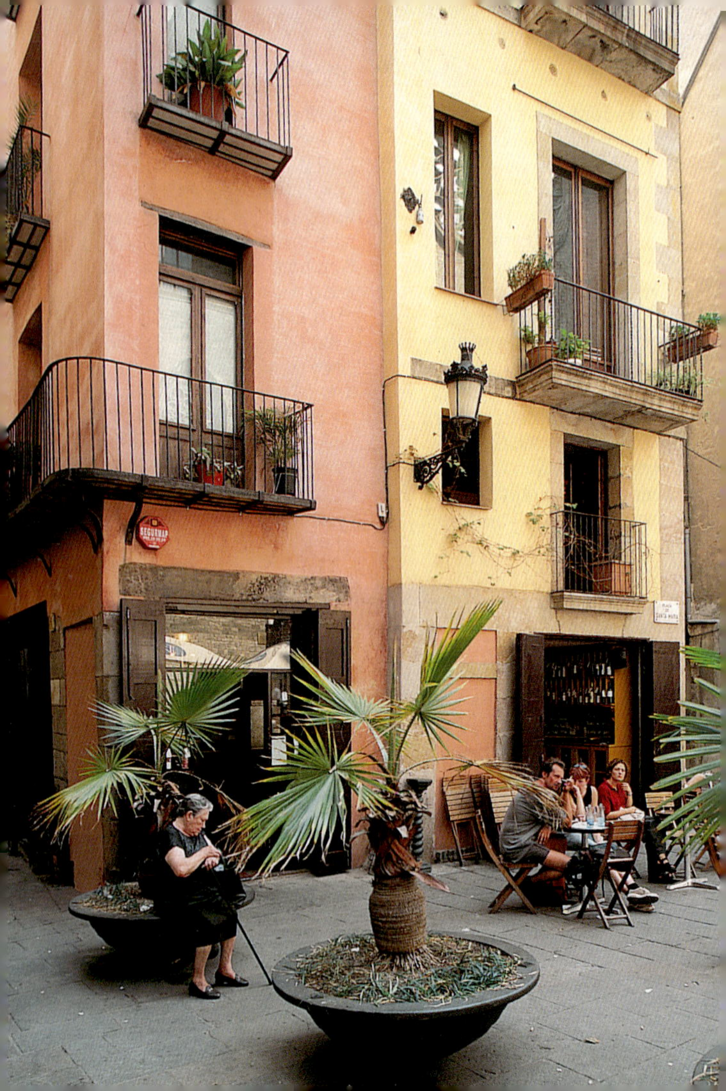
SEGURMAP

Ciutat Vella

studio was at C/de la Plata 3, now a restaurant.

The area is dominated by the baroque bulk of the **Església de la Mercè**, which contains Barcelona's most revered image of the Virgin.

A couple of blocks west, the attractive **Plaça Duc de Médiniceli** was designed by Francesc Molina, who also built the Plaça Reial. The column and fountain in the middle of the square, honouring a 14th-century Catalan admiral, is the first monument in Barcelona to be made from that favoured material of the industrial revolution, iron.

La Ribera Y–Z 1–2
- Metro: Jaume I

Beyond busy Via Laietana is the old maritime quarter of La Ribera (in the days before land reclamation, this was the waterfront). Vast tracts of it were knocked down in the 18th century to make way for the Ciutadella, built by the Habsburg rulers after the Catalans had sided against Madrid in the War of the Spanish Succession. Fortunately, some of the glories of the old district remain. In particular, **Carrer de Montcada** is a late-medieval gem, packed with splendid mansions dating back to the 15th century. Many of these now house prestigious museums, art shops and galleries.

Museu Picasso Z 2
- Metro: Jaume I
- C/Montcada 15–19
- Tel. 93 319 63 10
- Tues–Sat 10 a.m.–8 p.m.;
- Sun 10 a.m.–3 p.m.

Occupying three mansions, the museum has a staggeringly large collection of Picasso's work, with a wealth of paintings, sculpture, ceramics and graphics. It is strongest on three very different phases of the artist's long career—the early years from 1890 till 1904 when Picasso left Barcelona for Paris; his time as a mature Cubist around 1917; and the 1950s, with a large group of canvasses devoted to his intense re-working of Velasquez's *Las Meninas.*

Above all, the museum draws out the unstoppable creativity of the man. The early paintings reveal a dazzling precocity. His development from young art student to one of the greatest of modern artists takes place magically before your eyes. The extraordinary ability shown in Realist works such as the self

A quiet moment on Plaça de Santa Maria in the heart of the old Ribera district.

Sightseeing

portraits of 1896–97, the portraits of his parents and the assured *First Communion*, is matched only by the ease with which he abandoned all this and re-invented European art at the turn of the 20th century.

Museu Tèxtil i d'Indumentària Z 2

- Metro: Jaume I
- C/de Montcada 12
- Tel. 93 319 76 03
- Tues–Sat 10 a.m.–8 p.m.;
- Sun 10 a.m.–3 p.m.

This museum is housed in the fine 14th-century Palau de Liló. Enter through an elegant courtyard to displays of textiles dating back to the 4th century, together with collections of historic lace and embroidery, and fashion items ranging from the baroque era to the present.

Museu Barbier-Mueller d'Art Precolombí Z 2

- Metro: Jaume I
- C/de Montcada 14
- Tel. 93 310 45 16
- Tues–Sat 10 a.m.–8 p.m.;
- Sun 10 a.m.–3 p.m.

Next door is the Barcelona branch of a Swiss-based museum devoted to the indigenous art of South and Central America. The exhibitions change, with items rotating with the main museum in Geneva.

Santa Maria del Mar Z 3

- Metro: Jaume I
- Plaça de Santa Maria
- Tel. 93 310 23 90
- Open daily 9 a.m.–1.30 p.m., 4.30–8 p.m.

It's hard to believe now, but this superb Catalan-Gothic church at the end of C/de Montada overlooked the sea when building started in 1329. The restrained decor of the interior, with a magnificent 15th-century rose window at the south end, widely spaced Gothic arches and a dramatic fan-vaulted ceiling, is courtesy of Spanish Civil War anarchists, who set fire to the place in 1936 and burnt all its later baroque accretions.

Parc de la Ciutadella E 5

- Metro: Jaume I/Arc de Triomf

This pleasant park was laid out on the site of the hated Ciutadella: the Habsburg fortress was so big that when it was pulled down in the mid-19th century it took ten years to complete the task.
Today, the park contains something for everyone: a boating lake, the City Zoo, a winter garden and an elaborate ornamental fountain in neoclassical style, part of which was worked on by the young Antoni Gaudí, when he was still a student. The Catalonian Parliament

Ciutat Vella

is here, too, and occupies a remaining part of the Ciutadella, together with the Museum of Modern Catalonian Art. At the north end of the park lies the red-brick **Arc de Triomf**, designed for the 1888 Universal Exposition by Josep Vilaseca.

Museu de Zoologia E 5
- Metro: Jaume I/Arc de Triomf
- Passeig Picasso,
- Parc de la Ciutadella
- Tel. 93 319 69 12
- Tues–Sun 10 a.m.–2 p.m.;
- Thurs 10 a.m.–6.30 p.m.

In the northwest corner of the park, the museum of natural history is located in Domènech i Montaner's witty Modernista parody of a medieval castle, where stone has been replaced by the less stately brick and iron. It served as the café-restaurant for the 1888 Exposition, which mainly took place in this park, and is generally known as the *Castell dels Tres Dragons* (Castle of the Three Dragons).

Museu de Geología E 5
- Metro: Jaume I/Arc de Triomf
- Parc de la Ciutadella
- Tel. 93 319 6895
- Tues–Sun 10 a.m.–2 p.m.;
- Thurs 10 a.m.–6.30 p.m.

A large museum of geological items from the region, along with dinosaur and other fossils, many of which were found in the hills around Barcelona.

Museu d'Art Modern de Catalunya E 5
- Metro: Jaume I/Arc de Triomf/ Barceloneta
- Plaça d'Armes,
- Parc de la Ciutadella
- Tel. 93 319 57 28
- Tues–Sat 10 a.m.–7 p.m.;
- Sun 10 a.m.–3.30 p.m.

Located in the Parliament building in the centre of the park, this museum concentrates on Catalonian art from the 19th century up to the 1930s. It's inevitable, therefore, that among some fairly stodgy Romantic and Realist paintings, the vibrant work of the Modernista artists such as Santiago Rusiñol, Isidre Nonell and Ramon Casas should stand out. Among them is the famous painting by Casas that used to hang on the wall of *Els Quatre Gats*, featuring the artist and the owner of the restaurant, Pere Romeu, on a tandem.

The museum also has items of furniture by Gaudí, and works by Joaquim Sunyer and Xavier Nogués exemplifying the later *noucentista* school, which sought a more classical and less fantastical approach to art.

SHOPPING

The old city is still the place to look for antiques, antiquarian books and fine art—at a price. Catalan ceramics range from the primitive to the most sophisticated, and they're often highly original; specialist shops are scattered across the city, including a few half-hidden in the narrow streets behind the cathedral. Traditional and modern jewellery, hand-made rustic furniture in charming colours and other high quality craft goods, as well as some of the artisans who produce them may be found at the Poble Espanyol in Montjuïc. Embroidery, lace and woven rugs are made in mountain villages where the old patterns and skills are kept alive.

An intensive cottage industry produces leather goods, mainly handbags and clothing—jackets, skirts and trousers, boots and shoes. Spain's fashion designers have made a name for themselves in recent years; look for their creations in boutiques along the boulevards and in the arcades and galleries of the Eixample district. On Av. Diagonal 557, **L'Illa** is a huge mall where you can buy everything under the sun in no less than 140 shops and restaurants, including the book and music chain FNAC, and a splendid food hall. Further along the avenue at nos. 609–615, the **Pedralbes Centre** is another mall with an emphasis on fashion and accessories, art, decoration and gifts.

El Raval

EL RAVAL

The Raval lies like a mirror-image of the Barri Gòtic on the other side of La Rambla. In the 1920s and 30s the area was known as the Barrio Chino, a Chinatown with few Chinese but plenty of exotic lowlife, and the city's raciest red-light district. It's still a place to be careful at night, although time and the efforts of city planners have tamed it. In the backstreets you'll find some of Barcelona's most atmospheric bars and restaurants and a handful of sights that shouldn't be missed.

Centre de Cultura Contemporánia de Barcelona (CCCB) C 4
- Metro: Catalunya
- C/Montalegre 5
- Tel. 93 306 41 00
- June, July, August Tues–Sat 11 a.m.–8 p.m.;
- Sun and holidays 11 a.m.–3 p.m.
- Sept–May Tues, Thurs, Fri 11 a.m.–2 p.m.; 4 p.m –8 p.m.;
- Wed, Sat 11 a.m. –8 p.m.;
- Sun and holidays 11 a.m.–7 p.m.

This showpiece gallery holds temporary exhibitions of art and architecture, as well as showing films and putting on concerts. The building is a former workhouse and lunatic asylum, and its neoclassical shell is harmoniously juxtaposed with the high-tech, modern arts centre inside.

Museu d'Art Contemporani de Barcelona (MACBA) D 4
- Metro: Catalunya
- Plaça dels Àngels 1
- Tel. 93 412 08 10
- Mon, Wed–Sat 11 a.m.– 7.30 p.m; Sun 10 a.m.–3 p.m.

It rises out of the Raval like a mirage, so shimmering white among the dark old streets that it's almost blinding to look at in the midday sun. Designed by the American architect Richard Meier, the gallery concentrates on trends in international as well as Catalan art since the 1940s. Works on display are drawn from a huge collection and regularly changed. Artists to look out for include Miró, Klee and Rauschenberg, and home-grown talent such as Joan Brossa, Miquel Barceló and Susana Solano.

Antic Hospital de la Santa Creu W 4
- Metro: Liceu
- C/Carme 47–C/Hospital 56
- Mon–Fri 9 a.m.–8 p.m.;
- Sat 9 a.m.–2 p.m.

The institution ceased functioning as a hospital a century ago, and its beautiful colonnaded cloister is now used as a public garden. Part

Sightseeing

of the building houses the Catalonian National Library, while the fine Gothic chapel has been turned into a gallery for temporary art shows.

Sant Pau del Camp W 6
- Metro: Paral.lel
- C/Sant Pau 101
- Tel. 93 441 00 01
- Mon, Wed–Sun 11.30 a.m.–1 p.m., 6–7.30 p.m.;
- Tues 11.30 a.m.–12.30 p.m.

The squat tower of Barcelona's oldest church peeps out from among tall palm trees. It's mainly Romanesque in style and dates from the 12th century, when the area around here was open countryside and earned it the name of St Paul in the Fields.

Palau Güell C–D 5
- Metro: Liceu
- C/Nou de la Rambla 3–5
- Tel. 93 317 39 74
- Guided tours Mon–Sat
- 10 a.m.–2 p.m., 4–8 p.m.

Antoni Gaudí's first mature work, this extraordinary mansion was commissioned by the industrialist Eusebi Güell. Built in 1886–90, it is full of the master's trademark touches: a delight in materials like ceramic and wrought iron; the holistic approach to a building, with equal artistic importance given to its functional aspects; and an eclectic use of medieval and Ottoman influences. The highpoint is the wavy roof, whose forest of chimneys is decorated with pieces of broken ceramic tiles. This technique, known as *trencadis*, was first brought to Spain by the Arabs and triumphantly revived by Gaudí.

Museu Marítim C 5
- Metro: Drassanes
- Avda de les Drassanes
- Tel. 93 318 32 45
- Open daily 10 a.m.–7 p.m.

The Maritime Museum is housed in the city's most outstanding Catalan-Gothic secular building, the 13th–14th century Drassanes (shipyards). Beneath the huge stone-vaulted ceilings, whole ships were built and sent out to forge Catalonia's maritime empire in the Middle Ages. The museum contains displays on Barcelona's historic connection with the sea, information on Narcis Monturiol, the pioneer submariner, and some impressive model ships. The centrepiece is a full-size replica of the Royal Galley, Don John of Austria's flagship at the 1571 Battle of Lepanto.

The MACBA has three floors of modern painting and sculpture.

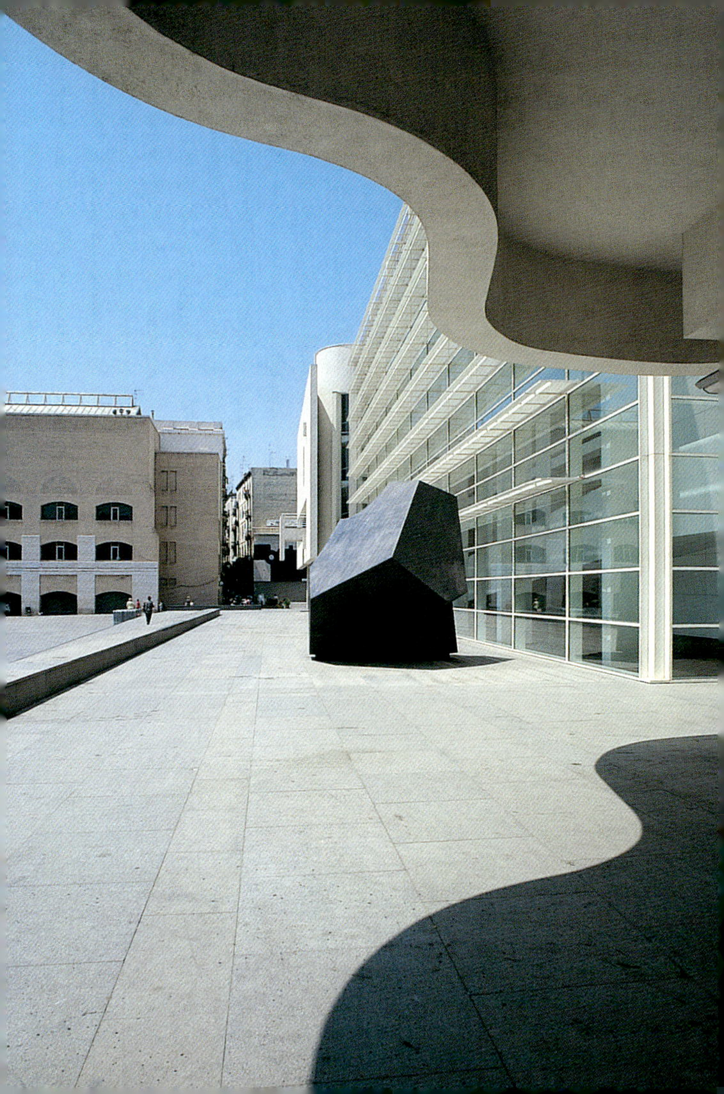

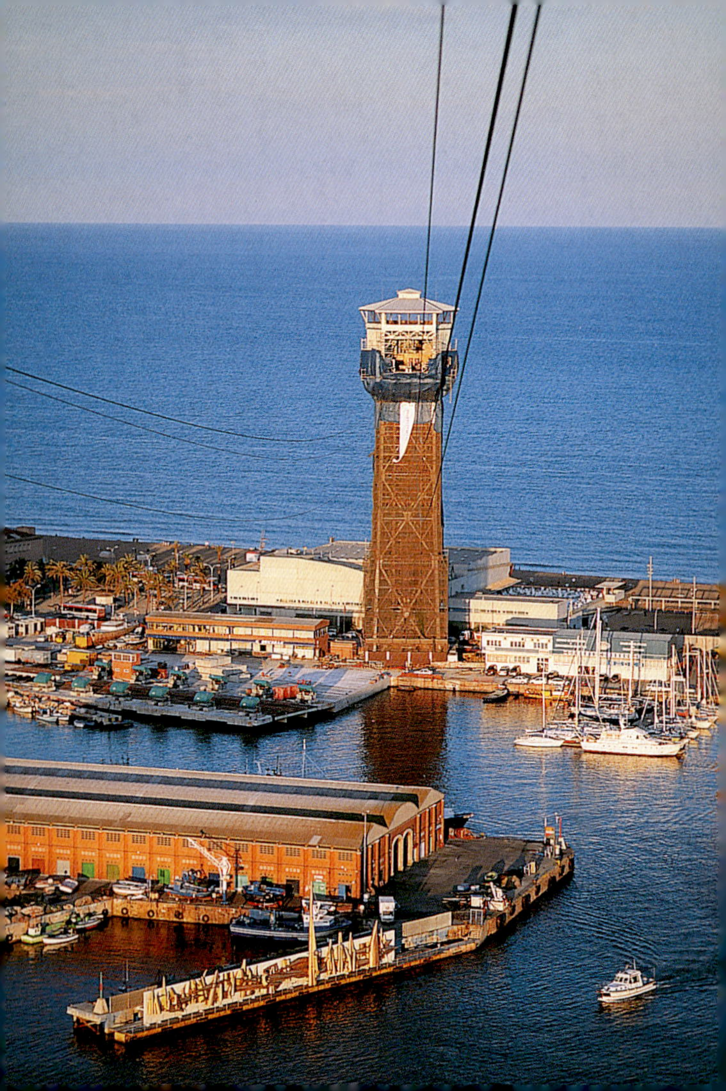

Waterfront

WATERFRONT

When the advent of container shipping in the 1960s and 70s forced the main port to move to a larger site a short distance along the coast, Barcelona's old port (Port Vell) soon fell into a state of decay. Since then, the transformation of around 3 km of city waterfront—including the creation of a swish harbourside restaurant area for the 1992 Olympics—has been little short of miraculous. These days it forms one of the city's liveliest and most extensive entertainment and leisure spots. What's more, with the beaches now thoroughly cleaned up as well, there's excellent bathing to be enjoyed just a stone's throw from the city centre.

Port Vell D 6
- Metro: Drassanes/Barceloneta

The old port lies just south of the Columbus Monument. You can take a **Golondrina** boat trip around the harbour; the boats depart from Moll de la Fusta. The main Port Vell development is out on the Moll d'Espanya quay, reached by a floating wooden gangway called

A cable car links Port Vell to Montjuic.

the **Rambla de Mar**. The massive **Maremàgnum** leisure centre, with its spectacular curving mirror entrance, boasts an enormous range of shops, restaurants and nightclubs. Just behind it is a superb aquarium, a replica of Monturiol's 19th-century wooden submarine and an **IMAX** cinema, showing giant-format films.

Aquàrium de Barcelona D 6
- Metro: Drassanes/Barceloneta
- Moll d'Espanya, Port Vell
- Tel. 93 221 74 74
- Open daily 9.30 a.m.–9 p.m.;
- July and August 9.30 a.m.–11 p.m.

Divided into 21 separate aquariums, this can rightly claim to be the world's best collection of Mediterranean marine life. It's a great place to take the kids, and the 80-m tunnel through the shark tank is sure to prove a spine-tingling favourite.

Museu d'Història de Catalunya D 5
- Metro: Barceloneta
- Palau de Mar, Plaça de Pau Vila 3
- Tel. 93 225 47 00
- Tues, Thurs, Fri, Sat 10 a.m.–7 p.m.;
- Wed 10 a.m.–8 p.m.; Sun and holidays 10 a.m.–2.30 p.m.

The huge Palau de Mar warehouse sits across the Port Vell harbour. It was converted into a prestige

museum devoted to the history of the region at considerable expense and opened in 1996. Starting with the pre-Roman Iberian tribes, it gives a resolutely Catalan's-eye view of events through to modern times, with some interactive exhibits that allow you to try on armour, dive into a Civil War air-raid shelter and so on.
Finding a good place for refreshments poses little problem here. There's a 4th-floor café with a superb terrace overlooking Port Vell, while the harbourside arcades below have a string of good-quality fish restaurants.

Barceloneta D–E 6
Metro: Barceloneta

Behind the Palau de Mar, Barceloneta—"Little Barcelona"—was built in the mid-18th century to a design of the French military engineer Prosper Verboom. He had also been responsible for the construction of the Ciutadella, and this grid of straight-as-a-die streets and tenement housing was intended for the inhabitants of La Ribera who had been displaced by the fortress. With its dilapidated façades, intimate local cafés and rows of washing hanging out of windows to dry, it has somehow managed to keep its earthy working-class character; as a maritime district, it also prides itself on possessing excellent seafood restaurants, which are worth bearing in mind if you're heading for a day out on the beaches just beyond.

Port Olímpic E–F 6
Metro: Cuitadella-Vila Olímpica

The Passeig Marítim beachfront promenade leads from Barceloneta to the city's newest grand project in urban planning. Until recently, this area was cut off from the rest of Barcelona by disused factory sites and obsolete railway lines, but was redeveloped with breathtaking energy and elan for the 1992 Olympic Games. Two thousand apartments in the **Vila Olímpica** were built to house the athletes, and a glamorous **marina** created for the sailing events. The apartments are now privately owned and much sought after, and the marina is a popular hangout for the Barcelonese, who come here for the bars, nightlife and wall-to-wall fish restaurants. Just back from the marina are the city's tallest skyscrapers, the Hotel Arts and the Torre Mapfre. The leisure complex next to them has shops, the Gran Casino, a Planet Hollywood restaurant and the eye-catching *Peix,* Frank Gehry's gigantic copper fish.

Montjuïc

MONTJUÏC

The large hill west of the city centre was for centuries used by the military because of its natural strategic advantages, and on more than one occasion the armies of the Madrid kings bombarded the citizens of Barcelona from its heights to keep them in line. Earlier, the Romans had a temple here, and there was a medieval Jewish cemetery too, leading to a debate among historians as to whether Montjuïc's name comes from "Mount of the Jews" or "Mount Jove". It has never been a residential area, and there are few cafés or restaurants. But it makes up for this by being home to some of Barcelona's best museums and most scenic viewpoints. The climb up is pretty steep. You can choose easier options such as the funicular railway, the Telefèric cable-car, the bus from Plaça d'Espanya, or a series of escalators at the foot of the Palau Nacional.

Castell de Montjuïc/ Museu Militar B 6
Metro: Paral.lel, then Funicular and Telefèric de Montjuïc/Bus 50
Parc de Montjuïc
Tel. 93 329 86 13
Tues–Fri 9.30 a.m.–6.30 p.m.;
Sat, Sun 9.30 a.m.– 7.30. p.m.

The Castell is at the southern end of Montjuïc, overlooking both town and sea. Dating from the 17th century, it has a bloody history as the place where Barcelona's radicals were tortured and executed, from the anti-Bourbon rebels of the War of the Spanish Succession right up to the Civil War republicans of the 1930s. It is now a military museum, with an extensive collection of swords, pikes, ancient guns, toy soldiers and a picture gallery of military figures and historic battles—there's even an equestrian statue of General Franco that has somehow avoided destruction. You'll also find a café in the courtyard, and a 360° view of Barcelona from the castle battlements.

Fundació Joan Miró B 5
Metro: Paral.lel, then Funicular de Montjuïc/Bus 50
Plaça Neptú, Parc de Montjuïc
Tel. 93 329 19 08
July–Sept Tues–Sat 10 a.m.– 8 p.m.; Thurs 10 a.m.–9.30 p.m.;
Sun 10 a.m.–2.30 p.m.;
Oct–June Tues–Sat 10 a.m.– 7 p.m.; Thurs 10 a.m.–9.30 p.m.;
Sun 10 a.m.–2.30 p.m

You can take a cable car back to the Funicular station, from where it's a short walk to this beautiful modern gallery, custom-built in the

Sightseeing

The Fundació Joan Miró displays works by the great painter and his contemporaries.

1970s to display the works of local boy, Joan Miró (1893–1983). The collection gathers together paintings, sculptures and tapestries from all periods of the artist's long life, and provides an unrivalled opportunity to encounter Miró's special blend of the surreal and the abstract. There's also a small group of works by Miró's contemporaries such as Henry Moore, Matisse and Alexander Calder, whose *Mercury Fountain* sculpture was first shown at the Republican pavilion alongside Picasso's *Guernica* during the Paris Exhibition of 1937.

Museu Etnològic B 5
- Metro: Poble Sec
- Passeig de Santa Madrona
- Tel. 93 424 68 07
- Tues, Thurs 10 a.m.–7 p.m.;
- Wed, Fri–Sun 10 a.m.–2 p.m.

The Ethnology Museum has an impressive collection of non-European cultural artefacts from as far afield as South America, India, Japan and Aboriginal Australia.

Museu d'Arqueología B 5
- Metro: Poble Sec
- Passeig de Santa Madrona 39–41
- Tel. 93 424 65 77

Montjuïc

Tues–Sat 9.30 a.m.–7 p.m.;
Sun 10 a.m.–2.30 p.m.
The archaeological museum is located in one of the buildings on Montjuïc erected for the 1929 Exhibition. Inside are displays of objects found mainly in Catalonia, including items from the Greek, Roman and Visigoth eras. There's also an interesting section with Carthaginian jewellery and sculpture discovered in the Balearic Islands.

Anella Olímpica A 5
(Olympic Ring)

Metro: Paral.lel, then Funicular de Montjuïc/Bus 50

Behind a huge neoclassical façade, the **Estadi Olímpic** was originally built for the 1929 Exhibition, and then dramatically revamped to become the centrepiece of the 1992 Olympic Games. It is now the home venue of Barcelona's other football team, Espanyol.
The modernistic terrace next to the stadium is dominated by the elegant line of the white **Telefònica tower** and the glazed ceramic dome of the **Palau Sant Jordi**, a sports and concert arena designed by Japanese architect Arata Isozaki. Back on Avda Estadi, you can go for a dip in the Olympic pool at the **Bernat Picornell** swimming baths.

Museu Nacional Art de Catalunya (MNAC) B 4–5

Metro: Espanya, then escalator
Palau Nacional,
Parc de Montjuïc
Tel. 93 225 47 00
Tues–Sat 10 a.m.–7 p.m.;
Wed 10 a.m.–8 p.m.;
Sun 10 a.m.–2.30 p.m.

You will have had glimpses of the Palau Nacional from all around Montjuïc. Its elaborate spires and domes give it the appearance of a grand Habsburg palace that has been transported here by mistake from Castile; in fact, it's a neo-baroque pastiche, thrown up for the 1929 Exhibition and intended for demolition once the party was over. The building won a reprieve, and today houses a marvellous collection of Romanesque and Gothic Catalan art.

The undoubted highlight is the Romanesque section. This splendid group of altar paintings and frescoes were rescued early in the 20th century from churches in the Catalan Pyrenees, where they were falling into decay. Their stylized Romanesque figures with elongated, cartoonish faces both pre-date and transcend a naturalistic approach to painting—and the effect in, for example, the 12th-century fresco of Christ Pantocrator from the church of

Sightseeing

Sant Climent de Taüll, is overwhelmingly powerful and direct. The Gothic collection pales a little in comparison, though works by artists such as Bernat Martorell (1400–52) and Jaime Huguet (1412–92)—note his exquisite *St George and the Princess*—more than justify the claim that this was a Golden Age of Catalonian culture.

PESETA WISE

If you're planning an all-out assault on Barcelona's splendid array of museums and galleries, then it's worth considering purchasing the **Barcelona Card**. This gives up to 50% reductions at all the main sites, as well as offering discounts at selected shops, restaurants, nightclubs and attractions such as the Tibidabo funfair, zoo, aquarium and Golondrines boat tours around the harbour. On top of this, there's free travel on buses and metro and 15% off the airport bus and Bus Turístic. The card costs 2,500 ptas for one day, 3,000 for two days and 3,500 for three days (children aged 6–15 pay 500 ptas less on each ticket). Tickets can be bought at the main city tourist office on Plaça de Catalunya, and at its branches in the Ajuntament on C/de Ciutat and Barcelona-Sants station.

Font Màgica de Montjuïc B 4
- Metro: Espanya
- Plaça d'Espanya
- Performances: late June–late Sept daily 8 p.m.–midnight, with music Thurs–Sun 9.30 p.m.– midnight
- Rest of the year: Fri and Sat 7–9 p.m.

The "magic" fountain is another amazing relic of the 1929 Exhibition. During a performance, smoke-like sprays of water and jets like fireworks are lit by pink, turquoise, red and white lights. If you're lucky, it will all happen in time to music, which might include anything from Whitney Houston to Rodrigo's *Concierto de Aranjuez*. It's as bizarre as anything in the Miró gallery and not to be missed.

Pavelló Mies van der Rohe B 4
- Metro: Espanya
- Avda Marqués de Comillas
- Tel. 93 423 40 16
- Open daily Apr–Sept 10 a.m.– 8 p.m.; Oct–Mar 10 a.m.–6 p.m.

The German contribution to the Exhibition, designed by the doyen of modernist architecture, Ludwig Mies van der Rohe, was reconstructed on the same site in 1986. The pavilion's hard purity of line and relentless rationalism was the way of the future when it was

Montjuïc

Beneath the domes of the National Palace is the city's most prestigious art collection.

first built, and marked a radical departure from Barcelona's vertiginous Modernista style.

Poble Espanyol A 4
Metro: Espanya
Avda Marqués de Comillas
Tel. 93 325 78 66
Mon 9 a.m.–8 p.m.;
Tues–Thurs 9 a.m.–2 a.m.;
Fri, Sat 9 a.m.–4 a.m.;
Sun 9 a.m.–midnight

The road next to the pavilion leads up to this extraordinary adjunct to the 1929 Exhibition, a "Spanish Village" exemplifying traditional architectural styles from around the country. Enter through a replica of the 12th-century gates of Ávila to the Plaza Mayor, the main square with a mix of mock-medieval and Renaissance buildings from Castile and Aragon. Beyond here are winding streets with Andalusian churches, Zaragozan towers and houses from every Spanish region, inhabited by craft and souvenir shops, bars and restaurants, even an internet café. It's all very kitsch of course, but with its car-free environment and pervasive sense of the unreal, the village is an intriguing and agreeable place to spend an hour or two.

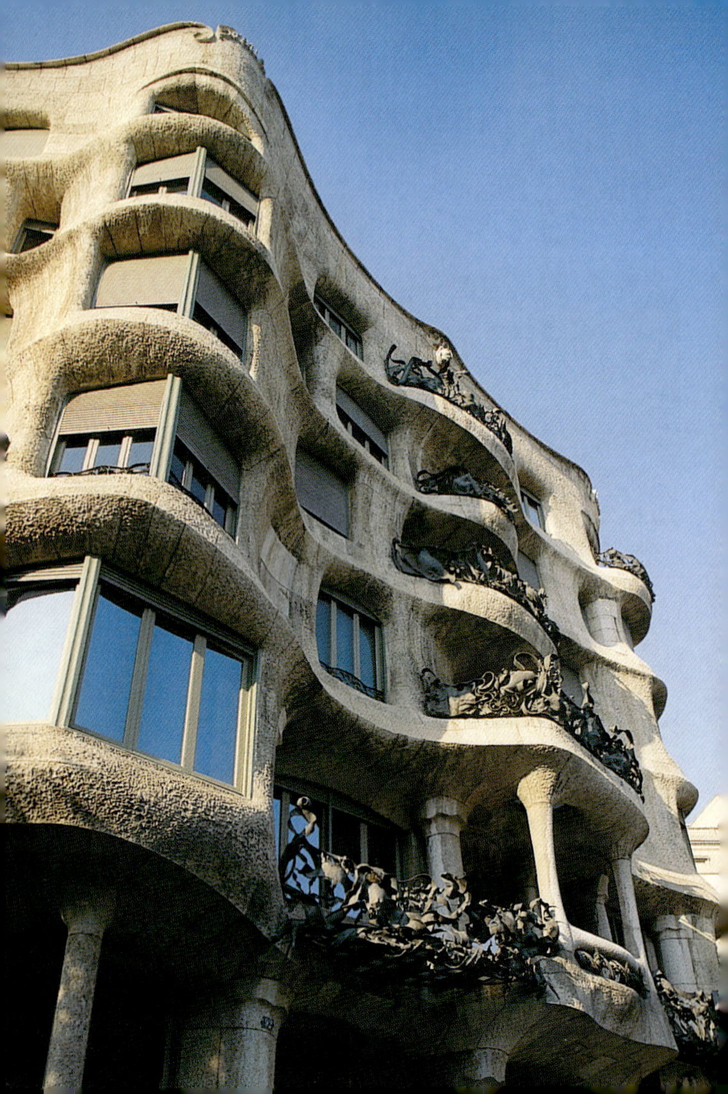

Eixample and Gràcia

EIXAMPLE AND GRÀCIA

Until the 1860s, Barcelona was restricted by the Madrid government from any expansion outside the city walls, and the land north of the old town was almost completely open country, with just an ancient dirt track leading up to the small village of Gràcia and the hills beyond. But a period of liberal rule under Isabel II saw the restrictions lifted and the face of Barcelona changed forever. The successful plan for the city's extension (*eixample*, in Catalan) was the work of Ildefons Cerdà, who came up with the vast geometrical pattern of grids, axes roads and boulevards that, by and large, became the Eixample we know today. Its relentless blocks are relieved by the presence of the best of Modernista architecture and Gaudí's final, incomplete masterpiece, the Sagrada Família church. Meanwhile, the district of Gràcia retains its village atmosphere, and a number of small squares, popular bars and restaurants make it a great place simply to wander around and explore.

Go up to La Pedrera's rooftop to discover the hidden chimneys, lined up like troops of aliens.

Plaça de Catalunya D 4
Metro: Catalunya

This massive square marks the border between the old town and the Eixample. Completed only in the 1920s, it is now the hub around which the city revolves—metro, FGC and mainline trains, airport and tourist buses all stop here, and it contains a good tourist information office. It is lined by a fairly uninspiring array of monumental buildings, though the **El Corte Inglés** department store is not only a useful landmark but also a great place for one-stop shopping, even if prices tend to be marginally high than other places. **El Triangle** at no. 4 is an enormous shopping complex with branches of Habitat, FNAC, the beauty product megastore Sephora and other specialty shops.

Passeig de Gràcia D 4
Metro: Catalunya/Passeig de Gràcia

The old road to Gràcia underwent a remarkable metamorphosis when the Eixample was built, and was re-invented as one of Europe's finest boulevards. Broad, tree-lined and with a range of pavement cafés to stop at, it's a superb place to promenade. Between the Gran Via and C/d'Aragó crossroads are a host of chic boutiques and smart jewellery shops, while in the Manzana de la Discòrdia and la Pedrera buildings it has the most concentrated burst of Modernista creativity anywhere in the city. At no. 96, the department store **Vinçon** contains three floors of the best home, garden and officeware, and has been prominent in promoting Barcelona as a "design" city. Even if you can't abide shops, look at the window displays, worth the trip alone.

Manzana de la Discòrdia D 3
- Metro: Passeig de Gràcia
- Passeig de Gràcia 35–45

The name given to the block just before C/d'Aragó is a pun on Block or Apple of Discord, because of the

---

MODERNISME IN BARCELONA

The cultural phenomenon known as Modernisme (Art Nouveau in France, Liberty in Italy and Jugendstil in Germany) flourished from around 1888 to 1910 and extended to all the arts—you can see Modernista paintings by Ramón Casas and Santiago Rusiñol at the Museum of Modern Art and read Modernista poetry by authors such as Joan Maragall. But without question, its one great outlet in Barcelona was in architecture. At least three architects of genius came to the fore during this period: Antoni Gaudí (1852–1926), Lluís Domènech i Montaner (1850–1923) and Josep Puig i Cadafalch (1867–1957). Characterized by an eclectic approach to style and the virtuoso mix of materials such as wrought iron, ceramics and brick, their buildings strove to achieve a total, "organic" effect, where every part of the structure was inseparable from the whole, as if it were a work of nature. It is in this spirit that, following nature's abhorrence of straight lines, Gaudí designed his famously wavy façades and rippling rooftops, and Domènech covered his sumptuous Palau de la Música Catalana with swirling floral motifs.

This burst of Modernista creativity was intense and relatively short-lived. The architects had depended on wealthy patrons willing to pay for their fantastic schemes, and such patrons had been in plentiful supply in Barcelona at the end of the 19th century. It was the age of resurgent Catalan nationalism, and they were fired with the belief that the great Modernista projects were part of a cultural renaissance not seen since the heyday of Barcelona's Gothic era. But by 1910 tastes had changed. The new fashion was for a more restrained, classically Mediterranean style. But the Modernista legacy lies all over town. In all, some 2,000 Modernista buildings were constructed, and the best of them still have the force to startle and confound our expectations of what a building should look like a century after they first appeared.

Eixample and Gràcia

fantastic incongruity of three of its buildings. They were designed by the three leading Catalan Modernista architects, and stand as a microcosm of the whole movement. Note that at present there is no public entry to the upper floors of any of them.

At no. 35, on the corner of C/de Consell de Cent, is Domènech i Montaner's **Casa Lleó Morera**. Dating from 1905, it has a highly embellished façade and Moorish-influenced turrets. The **Casa Amatller** is a couple of doors up at no. 41, designed by Puig i Cadafalch for a chocolate manufacturer named Antoni Amatller in 1898. The striking stepped gable is a gesture towards Flemish Renaissance style, though the exuberant use of polychrome ceramic tiles is pure Catalan Modernisme. Next door, and looking like one of Mr Amatller's colourful confectioneries that has been left in the sun, Gaudí's more immediately eyecatching **Casa Batlló** (1906) ostentatiously trumps its two neighbours.

The Casa Amatller also houses the new **Centre de Modernisme** where you can pick up a map pinpointing the full gamut of Barcelona's Modernisme legacy and purchase multi-tickets offering discounts and guided tours to many of them. There is also a small photographic exhibition showing parallel movements across the world.

Fundació Antoni Tàpies D 3
- Metro: Passeig de Gràcia
- C/Arago 255
- Tel. 93 487 03 15
- Tues–Sun 10 a.m.–8 p.m.

Take the first turning left to this gallery dedicated to the foremost living Catalan painter and sculptor Antoni Tàpies, who was born in Barcelona in 1923. It's located in a former publishing house built by Domènech i Montaner in 1880, and the red-brick façade is topped by a Tàpies sculpture that resembles an enormous piece of barbed-wire. It is in fact typical of his work, which is experimental, bold and often political—much of the early period is explicitly anti-Franco. The gallery also holds temporary exhibitions by other modern artists.

La Pedrera D 3
- Metro: Diagonal
- Passeig de Gràcia 92-C
- Tel. 93 484 59 95
- Open daily 10 a.m.–8 p.m.

This is one of Gaudí's best-known buildings. From the wavy façade to the tangled iron railings stuck onto the balconies like so many lumps of seaweed, there doesn't seem to be a straight line on show. Gaudí designed it as an apartment block for the wealthy developer Pere Milà and it's properly called Casa Milà—La Pedrera, meaning "The Stone Quarry", is a less-than-respectful descriptive nickname given to it by Barceloneses.

You can take a lift up to the **Espai Gaudí** in the attic, with displays and information about the architect's work, then climb up to the great, undulating roof, whose flamboyant chimneys and ventilators have had as much artistic attention lavished on them as any other part of the building. In summer, the roof is open on Friday and Saturday from 9 p.m. till midnight as the city's most spectacular terrace bar.

On the fourth floor, the **Pis de la Pedrera** is a reconstruction of how a Modernista-style apartment would have looked at the start of the 20th century.

Temple Expiatori de la Sagrada Família E 3

- Metro: Sagrada Família
- Plaça Sagrada Família–C/Mallorca 401
- Tel. 93 207 30 31
- Open daily Apr–Aug 9 a.m.–8 p.m.;
- Mar, Sept–Oct 9 a.m.–7 p.m.;
- Nov–Feb 9 a.m.–6 p.m.

The Church of the Holy Family (Sagrada Família in Catalan) was begun in 1882, but within two years the architect had resigned and the project was taken over by Antoni Gaudí. He worked on it till his death more than 40 years later, at which time it was still far from complete.

In many ways, this outlandish structure can be seen as an important affirmation of the continuing influence of Catalan Gothic in Barcelona. There are the familiar pointed Gothic arches, rose windows and immense spires—and yet, filtered through Gaudí's powerful Modernista imagination, nothing is quite as it seems. Look again and you'll see the spires are topped with frilly, multi-coloured flowers and the pinnacles erupt into bunches of fruit. Certainly, there's no other church like it, and it's almost impossible to see it and remain detached.

The Nativity Façade on the east side was the one Gaudí mostly worked on; the western entrance is through the Passion Façade, added since the 1950s. The crypt contains a museum devoted to the construction of the church, and you

Gaudí is buried in the crypt of his unfinished church.

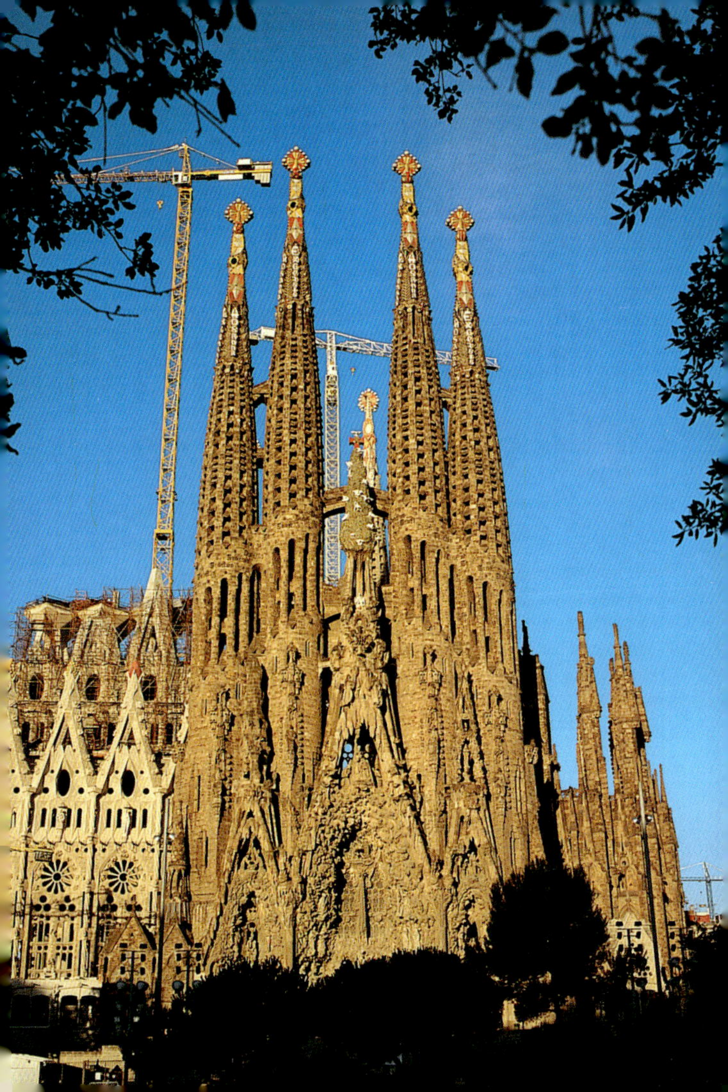

can go up one of the towers for fabulous views of the city. All fees contribute to the ongoing task of the Sagrada Família's completion, though it looks like it's going to take a long time.

Hospital Santa Creu i Sant Pau F 2–3
- Metro: Hospital de Sant Pau
- C/Sant Antoni Maria Claret 167

From the north end of the church, tree-lined Avda Gaudí leads up to another Modernista masterpiece, Domènech i Montaner's hospital complex, begun in 1900. It's a secular riposte to Gaudí's Sagrada Família and is certainly the only Modernista building to rival it in terms of size and scope. There are 48 pavilions, each with a different design and decorated with mosaics and murals, as well as fine grounds. It was built with a garden city in mind—Domènech sought an effect whose primary intention was to cheer up the patients. It should be noted that the pavilions (bar the main entrance) are not strictly open to the public, although nobody seems to mind if you take a discreet walk around their environs.

Gràcia D–E 1–2
- Metro: Joanic/Fontana

This once separate village long resisted absorption by Barcelona, a fate which was only sealed as recently as 1897, and its charming streets and squares still give the sense of being in another town. The best way to enjoy the district is to navigate between the main squares and just soak up the atmosphere. **Plaça de Ruis i Taulet** is the former town square, with a tall clocktower, town hall and a number of outdoor cafés. From here, you can head straight up to **Plaça del Sol**, a lively spot with some very popular local bars. A short distance northeastwards, **Plaça de la Virreina** is graced with the 17th-century church of Sant Josep. Northeast again, **Plaça de Rovira i Trias** is named after the architect whose plans for the Eixample were rejected. A bronze statue of him sits forlornly on a bench, the failed plans spread out on the pavement. On C/de les Carolines, you'll see the unmistakable imprint of Gaudí's genius on the façade of the **Casa Vicens**. It's a relatively restrained early work of 1883–88, though the Moorish-influenced tiling and superb wrought-iron fence are typically exuberant.

Parc Güell E 1
- Metro: Lesseps
- Bus 24, 25
- C/d'Olot
- Tel. 93 218 3811

Eixample and Gràcia

Open daily May–Aug 10 a.m.–9 p.m.;
Apr, Sept 10 a.m.–8 p.m.;
Mar, Oct 10 a.m.–7 p.m.;
Nov–Feb 10 a.m.–6 p.m.

When Eusebi Güell bought a large tract of hillside north of Gàrcia with the intention of developing it as a garden city, he asked his favourite architect to do the job. Gaudí began work on it in 1900, landscaping the park and designing the entrance and main public areas. But before any of the houses were built the project had collapsed, due to a lack of buyers willing to purchase any of the plots.

Perhaps what Gaudí had come up with was simply too far beyond the pale for its time. He was certainly at his most weird and wonderful here. The entrance pavilions are like fairy-tale gingerbread houses. From them, steps lead up to the great ceramic-encrusted lizard fountain, beyond which is a temple of 84 drunken columns. These support the park's centrepiece, an amazing "terrace in wonderland" edged with a vast, continuous and very crinkly bench, covered in *trencadis*, or broken tiles. It comes as no surprise to discover that this place haunted Catalonia's two famous surrealists, Salvador Dalí and Joan Miró. Fortunately, the city bought Güell's folly in 1922 and opened it to the public as a park. It extends a considerable distance up from the Gaudí terrace, and is in itself a lovely area of winding paths, shady woodland, and scenic views.

Casa-Museu Gaudí E 1

Bus 24, 25
Parc Güell, Carretera del Carmel
Open daily June–Sept 10 a.m.–7 p.m.;
Oct–May 10 a.m.–6 p.m.

Gaudí lived in a small house near the terrace while he was supervising the layout of the park. Inside are various items of furniture designed by both him and his assistant, Josep Maria Jujol, as well as other Gaudí memorabilia.

Museu del FC Barcelona A 1–2

Metro: Collblanc
Nou Camp, Avda Arístides Maillol
Tel. 93 496 36 08/37 69
Mon–Sat 10 a.m.–8.30 p.m.;
Sun 10 a.m.–2 p.m.

The seriousness with which Barcelonians take their football can be seen in the sheer scale of the local team's ground—seating 120,000 people, it's the largest in Europe. FC Barcelona—known to its fans as Barça—is one of the great names in world football, and this museum displays many of the trophies they have won over the

Sightseeing

Domènech i Montaner's project for the Santa Creu i Sant Pau hospital was completed after his death by his son Pere.

years, as well as vast quantities of other football memorabilia.

Museu de Ceràmica/Museu de les Arts Decoratives A 1
- Metro: Palau Reial
- Palau Reial de Pedralbes, Avda Diagonal 686
- Tel. 93 280 16 21 (Ceramics)
- Tel. 93 280 50 24 (Decorative Arts)
- Tues–Sun 10 a.m.–3 p.m.

These two museums are in the early 20th-century Palau Reial, which is in turn located inside an attractive park. The mansion was originally built for Gaudí's patron, Eusebi Güell, and acquired its royal title when King Alfonso XIII took possession of it in the 1920s (the stables and porter's lodge were designed by Gaudí, though all that's visible is the wrought-iron dragon gate on Avda Pedralbes). The Ceramics Museum has an excellent collection of ancient ceramic tiles, plates and tableware from around Spain, neatly arranged by region. There are also modern works by Picasso and Miró. The neighbouring Museum of Decorative Arts concentrates on furnishings and decorative objects from the early Middle Ages right up to the Modernista era.

Around Barcelona

AROUND BARCELONA

Spread out just beyond the city centre are some of Barcelona's most enjoyable sights. Getting to them is often half the fun, and you'll need to use the full range of public transport, including trains, buses, funicular railways and a picturesque ancient tram system.

Tibidabo
- FGC train to Avda Tibidabo, then Tramvia Blau and Funicular
- Tel. 93 211 79 42
- Open in summer Mon–Thurs noon–10 p.m.; Fri, Sat noon–1 a.m., Sun noon–10 p.m.; restricted hours at other times

The fun starts with the old Tramvia Blau ("Blue Tram") that rattles you along to the funicular station for the steep ride up Tibidabo. At 542 m, this is the highest of Barcelona's hills and on smog-free days the entire city is laid out spectacularly before you. Indeed, so splendid is the sight that it gave rise to Tibidabo's name, which is from the Latin for "all this I will give you"—the words used by the Devil to tempt Christ.

But the first thing you see as you get out of the funicular is the enormous **Basilica**, completed in 1940. There's a lift up to the roof, from where marvellous views extend out to the sea and inland over the forested north side of the mountain. Next to the funicular is the entrance to the **funfair**. This has various rides and attractions, including a ferris wheel, roller coaster and the Hotel Kruger, a house of horrors with more than a few surprises in store for the unwary.

Torre de Collserola
- Bus 211 from Tibidabo
- Tel. 93 406 93 54
- Wed–Sat 11 a.m.–2.30 p.m., 3.30–7 p.m.; Sun 11 a.m.–7 p.m.

Norman Foster's 288-m-high telecommunications tower was built so that the 1992 Olympics could be beamed around the world. You can take an external glass lift 115 m up to the observation deck, where the view extends for 70 km—or at least it does on one of those proverbial clear days.

Monestir de Pedralbes/Col.lecció Thyssen-Bornemisza
- FGC train to Reina Elisenda
- Biaxada del Monestir 9
- Tel. 93 280 14 34
- Tues–Sun 10 a.m.–2 p.m.

The monastery was founded in 1326 by Queen Elisenda, wife of Jaume II, and still houses a

Sightseeing

community of nuns. Immediately after the entrance is the beautiful, three-storey colonnaded cloister, one of the jewels of Catalan Gothic architecture. Just to the right, the Capella de Sant Miquel is covered with frescoes dating from 1346 by the Catalan artist Ferrer Bassa. You'll also find around the cloister a medieval pharmacy, the 15th-century refectory and kitchen, a Renaissance hospital and, back at the entrance, the Chapter House of 1419.

Occupying a former dormitory at the far end is the **Col.lecció Thyssen-Bornemisza**, part of a huge private collection acquired by Spain in 1993. Most of the collection is in Madrid, but Pedralbes is home to around 80 mainly religious works. There are some fine early Renaissance paintings by Andrea di Bartolo and Taddeo Gaddi, as well as canvasses by better-known masters such as Fra Angelico, Titian, Veronese, Lucas Cranach, and the Spaniards Zurbarán and Velázquez.

Colònia Güell

FGC train to Molí Nou
Santa Coloma de Cervelló
Tel. 93 640 29 36
Crypt under renovation.
Interior open for visits
Sun 10 a.m.–1.30 p.m.

In the attempt to quell increasing worker unrest in Barcelona, some of the wealthy elite sponsored industrial colonies away from the city. These were designed to be Catholic and conservative communities, where the owner would provide a miniature welfare state for his workers and in return the workers would, it was hoped, refrain from industrial disputes. The Colònia Güell was another of Eusebi Güell's grand schemes, and as with the doomed garden city in Barcelona (which became Parc Güell), this cloth-making colony out in the village of Santa Coloma eventually failed.

But once again, Antoni Gaudí was able to leave his mark on the place. He designed the church for the colony, and began work in 1899, but only the crypt was completed. On a pine-covered hill, it is typically surreal, and mysteriously organic, with curvy pews, tilting columns and an impressive brick version of a fan-vault ceiling, like nothing else in the world. It is also one of his most daring structures, and technically brilliant. Remarkably, there are no external buttresses or supports. The huge columns and ceiling are held up in a perfectly calculated tension, like a cat's-cradle raised to the level of architectural form.

Excursions

EXCURSIONS

There's an amazing diversity of things to see and do in such a pocket-sized region—you can hike in the High Pyrenees, bask on a Costa Brava beach, go wine-tasting in ancient vineyards and yet never be more than 150 km from Barcelona. The places recommended here are popular day trips from the city, and most can easily be reached by train or bus.

Girona

- RENFE train from Barcelona-Sants and Passeig de Gràcia stations

Northern Catalonia's largest city was founded by the Romans, for whom the location on a hill by the River Onyar made it perfect as a means of protecting the route from France to the south. Throughout the early part of its history it was at least as important as Barcelona, and the medieval walled city which you can see today contains some fine buildings from that period. The **cathedral**, with a baroque façade, stands at the top of a huge flight of 91 steps leading up from the Plaça de la Catedral. The church was begun in the 13th century and contains a vast Gothic nave that can claim to be one of the largest in the world. Look out too for the fine Romanesque cloister, adorned with sculptures representing figures of the Old Testament. In the Treasury, see the splendid Tapestry of the Creation, in its own room. Head down the steps again to reach the church of **Sant Feliu**. Its distinctive truncated tower is the result of a strike by lightning in 1581. The church itself marries Romanesque, Gothic and baroque styles. Nearby are the **Banys Àrabs**, Arab baths that are still in operation. They date from the 12th century, and so were in fact built long after the Arab occupation of the city. The architect was certainly influenced by Moorish design, however, and the baths stand as an unusual Moorish-Romanesque hybrid.

Leading south from Plaça de la Catedral, the Carrer de la Força runs through the **Call**, Girona's medieval Jewish district. You can get a flavour of how it once was at the **Centre Bonastruc Ça Porta**, an intriguing maze of rooms and stairways around an inner courtyard that stood at the centre of the Call. Finally, for an overview of Girona, climb to the **Passeig Arqueològic**, from where you can walk along the ancient walls and look out across the rooftops and church spires of the city.

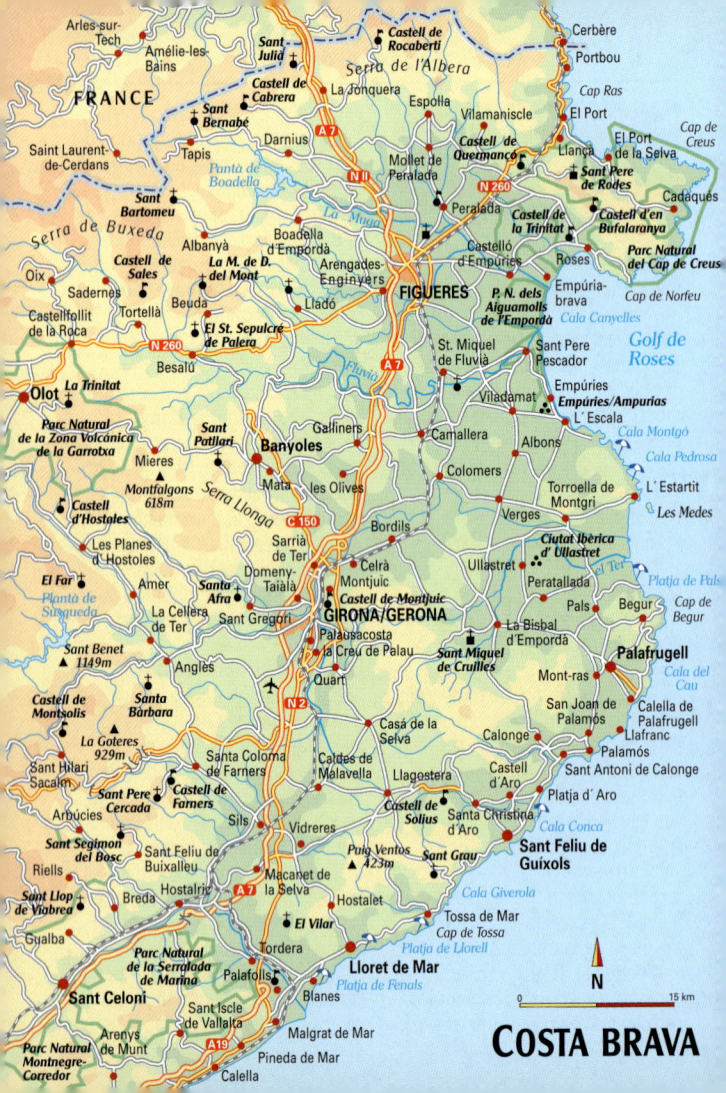

COSTA BRAVA

Excursions

Figueres

- RENFE train from Barcelona-Sants and Passeig de Gràcia stations
- Teatre-Museu Dalí open daily June 10.30 a.m.–5.45 p.m.; July–Sept 9 a.m.– 7.45 p.m.; Oct–May Tues–Sun 10.30 a.m.–5.45 p.m. Tel. 972 67 7500

This small town acts as a hub for the northern part of the Costa Brava. It has a bustling **Rambla**, the 18th century **Castell de Sant Ferran**, last stronghold of the Republicans at the end of the Spanish Civil War, and the **Museu de l'Empordà**, with Greek and Roman archaeological finds and a collection of Catalan art. But it would rarely rate a mention if it weren't for the birth here in 1904 of the great Surrealist painter and all-round eccentric, Salvador Dalí.

The **Teatre-Museu Dalí** was designed by the artist as a monument to his own fantastic vision of the world, something evident in every part of the museum, from the giant Dalíesque eggs on the outer walls to the bizarre installations inside. The paintings on display are drawn from all periods of Dalí's life, and include such typically unnerving challenges to normality as *The Spectre of Sex Appeal* and *Self-portrait with Fried Bacon*. In the *Sala de Mae West*, an entire room is designed as a grand portrait to the Hollywood actress, with the sofa as her lips, fireplaces as her nostrils and so on. Dalí died in Figueres in 1989, and as a final touch of the macabre was buried in his own museum.

Montserrat

- FGC train from Plaça Catalunya to Aeri de Montserrat, then cable car.
- Tourist Office: 93 87 77 77 77
- Basilica open daily 8 a.m.–10.30 a.m., noon–6.30 p.m.
- Museu de Montserrat open Mon–Fri 10 a.m.–6 p.m.; Sat, Sun 9.30 a.m.–6.30 p.m.

Montserrat lies 40 km northwest of Barcelona. Its name—which means "serrated mountain"—perfectly describes its appearance, a 1,200-m-high mass of jagged rock. In the 9th century, legend has it, the lost statue of the Black Virgin brought to Spain by St Peter was discovered here. Miraculously unable to be removed from the mountain, it was kept in place and a Benedictine monastery built around it instead. Perched dramatically on the side of the mountain and reached by a stunning cable-car ride, the current basilica dates from the 16th century, though it was severely

Sightseeing

damaged by Napoleon's troops in 1813 and had to be substantially rebuilt.

Montserrat is today one of Spain's pre-eminent pilgrimage sites and stands at the spiritual heart of Catalonia—its religious importance meant it was always able to retain its independence from Madrid, and the monks maintained Catalan as a language of learning even during the years of Franco's ban. The statue of the **Black Virgin** is above the high altar of the Basilica, and reached by a door to the right of the main entrance. If possible, you should also try to attend the daily Salve Regina at 1 p.m. or Vespers at 7 p.m., which are sung by the famous **Montserrat Boys' Choir**, the oldest in Europe. In one of the monastery buildings nearby is the **Museu de Montserrat**, with an interesting collection that contains archaeological finds, religious artefacts and paintings and sculptures by El Greco, Caravaggio, Picasso, Dalí and several Catalan artists.

Best of all, perhaps, are the scenic walks which you can take from the monastery and which afford fine panoramas of the surrounding countryside. You can also ascend higher up the mountain via a **funicular** to the Sant Joan hermitage. A brisk one-hour walk from here brings you to **Sant Jeroni** near the peak, where the views of Montserrat's great saw-tooth pinnacles are spectacular.

Alt Penedès

- RENFE train from Barcelona-Sants or Plaça Catalunya stations to Sant Sadurní and Vilafranca
- Bodegues Torres open Mon–Sat 9 a.m.–6 p.m.; Sun. 9 a.m.–2 p.m. Tel. 93 817 74 87.
- Caves Cordoníu: tours Mon–Fri 9–5 p.m., Sat, Sun 9 a.m.–1. p.m., Tel. 93 818 32 32.
- Tourist Offices: Sant Sadurni d'Anoia, Plaça de l'Ajuntament 1, baixos. Tel. 93 891 12 12. Vilafranca del Penedès, C/Cort 14. Tel. 93 892 03 58.

Catalonia's most productive wine region is the Alt Penedès, a mere 50 km west of Barcelona. This is where some of the country's best red and white wines hail from, and it's also the home of cava, Spain's version of champagne. Be warned that if you want to tour the vineyards, you'll probably be best off going by car.

The area's main town is **Vilafranca del Penedès**, where you can gain some preliminary knowledge of Catalan winemaking at the enjoyable Museu del Vi (Wine Museum). The town holds a wine

COSTA DAURADA

Sightseeing

festival each autumn to celebrate the grape harvest—the main events take place on the first Sunday in October.
A few kilometres to the northwest, the **Bodegues Torres** is the region's leading producer.
If it's *cava* you crave, head for nearby **Sant Sadurni d'Anoia**. The vineyards around here turn out almost all of the country's entire output. Just outside town, the **Caves Cordoniú** vineyard is worth heading for, and not just for its wine. The main building is a Modernista work designed by Puig i Cadafalch in the late 19th century. For more details on individual vineyards and visiting times, call the tourist offices.

Sitges
- RENFE train from Barcelona-Sants and Passeig de Gràcia stations.
- Museums open summer Tues–Sun 10 a.m.–9 p.m.; restricted times in winter.

Sitges is 40 km south of Barcelona on the Costa Daurada and one of Spain's liveliest Mediterranean resorts, boasting a famously high-energy nightlife. The town first came to the world's attention in the 1890s, when the Modernista painter Santiago Rusiñol set up a studio here that attracted followers from Barcelona's art set. Sitges's second wave of popularity started in the 1960s when it gained its current reputation as a hedonistic party town. It's popular with a wide range of people, from trendy Barceloneses to holidaying families as well as also being one of the biggest gay destinations in Europe. By day, the action centres on the resort's string of nine sandy beaches. You can survey them all by taking a stroll along the **Passeig Marítim** seafront promenade. But if the beach culture gets too hot to handle, you'll find the town has plenty to recommend it. The city end of the promenade leads to the 17th-century baroque church of **Sant Bartomeu i Santa Tecla**, near which is a street of beautiful old whitewashed houses. Here, too, is the **Museu Cau Ferrat**, based in Rusiñol's former studio on C/Fonollar. The house contains several of the artist's paintings, plus an assortment of drawings and other *objets d'art* that he collected. At the nearby **Museu Maricel del Mar** there are artworks from the medieval period onwards, and a fine collection of Catalan ceramics.

Tarragona
- RENFE train from Barcelona-Sants and Passeig de Gràcia stations

Excursions

The hilltop town of Tarragona was founded by the Romans in the 3rd century BC, and it was their principal city in this part of Spain. As such, it has a far greater collection of Roman remains than Barcelona. Down towards the sea is the **Amfitheatre**, once the site of gladiatorial combat. Roman sports fans would also be found at the **Circ Roma**, whose ruins are just above the amphitheatre, and which was where chariot races took place. At the southern end of the old town, the **Museu Nacional Arqueològic** has a vast collection of Roman finds, including a magnificent group of mosaics. The ticket also gives admission to the **Necropolis**, a little to the west of the town.

At the centre of Tarragona is a splendid tangle of medieval streets, many of whose houses are partly constructed from earlier Roman stonework. They lead to the great **Catedral**, built from the 12th–13th centuries, whose impressive façade demonstrates an effortless transition from Romanesque to Gothic. The cathedral's cloister is also a fine expression of this, with Gothic arches and Romanesque capitals. From the cathedral, work your way round to the **Passeig Arqueològic**, which gives fantastic views of the sea and the city, and runs between the original Roman walls and those erected by the British during the War of the Spanish Succession 2,000 years later.

Port Aventura

RENFE train from Barcelona-Sants and Passeig de Gràcia stations

Near the resort of Salou, this theme park, run by Universal Studios, was the first on such a big scale in Spain when it opened in 1995. It offers some of the most exciting rides in the world, including the infamous Dragon Khan, Europe's biggest roller coaster. The park aims to be educational as well as fun, with activities combining cultural information and cutting-edge technology. It is divided into "villages" representing the American Wild West, Polynesia, China, the Mediterranean and Mexico, all with their themed rides, shows and restaurants. A little train transports you from one to the other. The highlights, apart from the roller coaster in China, are shooting the rapids in the Wild West, exploring underwater in Polynesia's Sea Odyssey, marvelling at the Maya ruins in Mexico, and chilling out in a whitewashed Mediterranean fishing village, with a typical seafood meal.

Dining Out

Restaurants are on the whole good value in Barcelona, and you can usually eat as well at a small local taverna as at a fancy hotel. At lunchtime, be sure to check out the *menú del dia*, two or three courses plus wine and bread which most restaurants offer at a surprisingly low price. The following recommendations are marked with the $ sign to give some idea of what you might expect to pay per head for a three-course evening meal excluding drinks: $ budget price
$$ 2,500–5,000 ptas (15–30 euros)
$$$ more than 5,000 ptas (30 euros).

LA RAMBLA AND CIUTAT VELLA

Amaya
Metro: Liceu
La Rambla 20–24
Tel. 93 302 10 37
Open daily 1–5 p.m.,
8.30 p.m.–midnight
Well-known Basque restaurant specializing in fish dishes. Tables out on La Rambla. $$

Can Culleretes
Metro: Liceu
C/Quintana 5
Tel. 93 317 30 22
Tues–Sat 1.30–4.00 p.m.,
9–11 p.m., Sun 1.30–4 p.m.
Barcelona's oldest restaurant was founded in 1786. Superb traditional Catalan cuisine—the *espinacs a la Catalunya* (spinach lightly fried in olive oil with pine nuts, bacon, raisins and garlic) is sensational—and reasonably priced wines. $$

Los Caracoles
Metro: Dressanes
C/Escudellers 14
Tel. 93 302 31 85
Open daily 1 p.m.–midnight
Something of an institution, and easily detected in the narrow streets of the Barri Gòtic by the aroma emanating from chickens roasting on spits outside. Good seafood, snails (after which the restaurant is named), chicken. $$

Clàssic Gòtic
Metro: Jaume I
C/de la Plata 3
Tel. 93 319 92 98
Tues–Sat 7 p.m.–12.30 a.m,
Sun 1–4.30 p.m.

Dining Out

A touch touristy, with live music and a floor show—but then the cooking is high quality and the fine 16th-century building is where Picasso had his first studio. $$

La Locanda
- Metro: Urquinaona
- Dr. Joaquim Pou 4
- Tel. 93 317 46 09
- Tues–Sun 1 p.m.–4.30 p.m, 8 p.m.–12.30 a.m.

La Locanda's modern Italian cuisine consists of many specialities unavailable elsewhere, including some very Milanase risottos and beef or tuna carpaccios. $–$$

Mesón Jesús
- Metro: Liceu
- C/Cecs de la Boqueria 4
- Tel. 93 317 46 98
- Mon–Fri 1–4p.m., 8–11 p.m., Sat 1–4 p.m.

Atmospheric, old-fashioned taverna right by Santa Maria del Pi. $

Peimong
- Metro: Jaume I
- C/Templaris 6–10
- Tel. 93 318 28 73
- Tues–Sun 1–4.30 p.m., 8–11.30 p.m

For a break from the local cuisine, try some gutsy Peruvian cooking—the Papa Rellena starter, a twice-baked potato stuffed with egg, beans, olives and veal, is for those with an appetite the size of the Andes. $

Els Quatre Gats
- Metro: Catalunya
- C/Montsió 3bis
- Tel. 93 302 41 40
- Mon–Sat 9 a.m.–2 a.m., Sun 4 p.m.–1 a.m.

A Modernista landmark: the building is by Puig i Cadafalch, the restaurant was once frequented by artists such as Ram Santiago Rusiño cover was desi café at the fro restaurant at ti

Les Quinze Nit
- Metro: Liceu
- Plaça Reial 6
- Tel. 93 317 30 75
- Open daily 1–3.45 p.m., 8.30–11.30 p.m.

A modern approach to Catalan and Spanish cuisine that has proved very popular with locals. Reservations aren't taken, so arrive early to avoid queues. $$

Restaurant Pitarra
- Metro: Jaume I
- C/d'Avinyó 56
- Tel. 93 301 16 47
- Mon–Sat 1–4 p.m., 8.30–11 p.m.

Dining Out

This cosy restaurant has a lovely old interior whose walls are lined with paintings. The quality of the Catalan cuisine is famously high. $$

El Salón
- Metro: Jaume I
- C/Hostal d'en Sol 6–8
- Tel. 93 315 21 59
- Mon–Sat 2–5 p.m., 8.30 p.m.–00.30 a.m.

Stylish décor and rich, French-influenced cooking. Booking advisable. $–$$

Self Naturista
- Metro: Catalunya
- C/Santa Anna 13–15
- Tel. 93 318 23 88
- Mon–Sat 11.30 a.m.–10 p.m.

In a town dedicated to the munching of meat and fish, vegetarians will find this self-service place near Plaça Catalunya something of a relief. The dishes are imaginative, and there's always a good-value *menú del día*. $

Taxidermista
- Metro: Liceu
- Plaça Reial 8
- Tel. 93 412 45 36
- Tues–Sun 1.30–4 p.m., 8.30–11.30 p.m.

Elegant restaurant for the cool Plaça Reial crowd, serving Catalan and international cuisine in a former taxidermist's shop. $$–$$$

EL RAVAL

El Convent
- Metro: Liceu
- C/Jerusalem 3
- Tel. 93 317 10 52

ON THE MENU

Like much else in Barcelona, lunch and dinner are occasions which start later and continue longer than in many other major business cities. There's a wide and thriving range of international and Spanish regional restaurants, but the culinary highlight of any visit is the chance to sample deliciously earthy Catalan cuisine. Popular ingredients are fish and meat, accompanied by one of Catalonia's famous sauces such as *sofregit*, based on onion, tomato and garlic; *samfaina*, made with tomato, onion, garlic, pepper and aubergine; *picada*, which uses ground almond, crushed pine or hazel nuts, garlic, parsley and breadcrumbs; and *all i oli*, a fresh garlic mayonnaise. The Catalans are also keen on big, flavoursome salads, *botifarra* pork sausage served with white beans, and that homely national favourite *pa amb tomàquet*—bread rubbed with tomato.

Dining Out

Mon–Sat 1–4 p.m.,
8 p.m.–midnight
This restaurant is a long-standing favourite with diners in the Raval, who come here to enjoy the excellent range of Catalan dishes available, as well as the convivial atmosphere. $$

La Gardunya
Metro: Liceu
C/Jerusalem 18
Tel. 93 302 43 23
Mon–Sat 1–4 p.m.,
8 p.m.–midnight
At the back of La Boqueria market, this 19th-century inn is widely acclaimed for serving only the freshest ingredients. Their paellas are especially tasty. Quieter upstairs. $$–$$$

Restaurant España
Metro: Liceu
Hotel España
C/de Sant Pau 9–11
Tel. 93 318 17 58
Open daily 1–4 p.m.,
8.30 p.m.–midnight
The traditional Catalan cuisine is solid, if rather uninspiring, though that's more than made up for by consuming it in Domènech i Montaner's fantastic Modernista salon. The very affordable lunchtime *menú del día* is worth checking out. $$

Restaurante Romesco
Metro: Liceu
C/de l'Arc de Sant Agusti
Tel. 93 318 93 81
Mon–Sat 1 p.m.–00.30 a.m.
Near to the Hotel España, this cheap-and-cheerful little spot is good for chicken, squid and octopus. $

Silenus
Metro: Catalunya
C/dels Angels 8
Tel. 93 302 26 80
Mon–Sat 1–4 p.m., 9–11.30 p.m.
A sophisticated Catalan-Spanish based menu in a trendy restaurant near the MACBA gallery. $$

WATERFRONT

Agua
Metro: Ciutadella–Vila Olímpica
Pg. Marítim de la Barceloneta 30
Tel. 932 251 272
Daily 1.30 p.m–4 p.m,
8.30 p.m–1.30 a.m
Your best bet in the touristy Olympic Village area. An up market, split-level restaurant that offers a beautiful view of the Mediterranean and innovative fish dishes. $$

Can Ramonet
Metro: Barceloneta
C/Maquinista 17
Tel. 93 319 30 64

If you just want a sandwich, look out for the Bocadillos sign.

Mon–Sat 10 a.m.–4 p.m., 8 p.m.–midnight
Excellent seafood in one of the oldest parts of Barceloneta. $$–$$$

Can Ros
Metro: Barceloneta
C/Almirall Aixada 7
Tel. 93 221 45 79
1–5 p.m., 8 p.m.–midnight. Closed Wed all day and Mon night.
Another superb Barceloneta fish restaurant, serving delicious paella and sumptuous black *arròs negre*, seafood cooked with rice in squid ink. $$

Can Solé
Metro: Barceloneta
C/de Sant Carles 7
Tel. 93 221 50 12
Mon–Sat 1–4 p.m., 8 p.m.–midnight
Simple but classy fish dishes. The desserts are legendary. $$–$$$

Paco Alcalde
Metro: Barceloneta
C/Almirall Aixada 12
Tel. 93 221 50 26
Mon, Wed–Sun 1 p.m.–2 a.m.
Friendly local *bodega*, with good seafood tapas to accompany the wine. $$

Dining Out

Els Pescadores
- Metro: Poble Nou
- Plaça Prim 1
- Open daily 1–3.45 p.m., 8 p.m.–midnight

Located on a delightful square in the old fishing village of Poble Nou. You can expect marvellously fresh fish, cooked in the best modern Catalan style. $$$

Set Portes
- Metro: Barceloneta
- Passeig Isabel II 14
- Tel. 93 319 30 33
- Open daily 1 p.m.–1 a.m.

Stylish restaurant that's remained largely unchanged since its foundation in 1836. The Set Portes ("seven doors") has an extensive menu of Catalan specialities and a hunger-busting range of paellas. It's a great favourite with locals and tourists alike, so booking is advisable for evenings. $$–$$$.

MONTJUÏC

La Bodegueta
- Metro: Poble Sec
- C/Blai 47
- Tel. 93 442 08 46
- Tues–Sun 1.30–4 p.m., 8.30 p.m.–midnight

This classic local Poble Sec restaurant, complete with red-checked tablecloths and walls lined with wine barrels, has great *escalivada*, a filling mix of aubergine, red pepper and onions on a thick slice of bread. $

Miramar
- Metro: Paral.lel, then Funicular de Montjuïc/Bus 50
- Avda Miramar
- Tel. 93 442 31 00
- Open daily except Wed in summer 10 a.m.–2 a.m., winter 10 a.m.–midnight

There aren't many places to chill out with a drink and a snack on Montjuïc itself, but this café triumphantly steps into the breach, with panoramic portside views. $

Museu Nacional Art d'Catalunya Café
- Metro: Espanya, then escalator
- Palau Nacional
- Tel. 93 225 50 07
- Tues–Sat 10 a.m.–7 p.m., Sun 10 a.m.–2 p.m.

Good sandwiches as well as an à la carte menu and a decent *menú del día* make this the lunch-stop of choice for discerning visitors to the museums of Montjuïc. $–$$

La Parra
- Metro: Hostafrancs
- C/Joanot Martorell 3
- Tel. 93 332 51 34
- Tues–Fri 8.30 p.m.–midnight,

Sat 2–4.30 p.m.,
8.30 p.m.–midnight,
Sun 2 –4.30 p.m.
Just beyond Plaça Espanya, this 200-year-old establishment is strong on Catalonia's traditional rural cuisine, with huge portions of meat, game and fish cooked over a charcoal grill. $$–$$$

EIXAMPLE AND GRÀCIA

Botafumeiro
Metro: Fontana
C/Gran de Gràcia 81
Tel. 93 218 42 30
Open daily 1 p.m.–1 a.m.
Treat yourself to what is generally agreed to be the best shellfish in Barcelona—though with appropriately high prices. $$$

Bracafé
Metro: Catalunya
C/Casp 2
Tel. 93 302 30 82
Open daily 7 a.m.–10.30 p.m (Saturday until midnight)
Well-known Eixample haunt. It's great for a leisurely breakfast, with excellent coffees, pastries and other snacks. $

La Dama
Metro: Diagonal
Avda Diagonal 423
Tel. 93 202 06 86
Open daily 1–3.30 p.m.,
8.30–11.30 p.m.
Refined Catalan cuisine presented with considerable panache in resolutely upmarket ambience. $$$

El Glop
Metro: Fontana
C/ St. Luis 24
Tel. 93 213 70 58
Open daily 1–5 p.m.,
8 p.m.–1 a.m.
Fast-paced and ever-popular, this enjoyable taverna specializes in char-grilled meats, and is also a good place for *torrades*, the toasted version of *pa amb tomàquet*. There are branches at La Rambla 65 and C/Casp 21. $–$$

Madrid-Barcelona
Metro: Passeig de Gràcia
C/Aragó 282
Tel. 93 215 70 26
Mon–Sat 1–3.30 p.m.,
8.30–11.30 p.m.
This was once a café at a station on the Madrid train line that ran along the street here. It boasts a fine interior from the early 20th century, and a solid Catalan-international menu.

Maria Cristina
Metro: Diagonal
C/de Provença 269
Tel. 93 215 32 37

Dining Out

Mon–Fri 1.30–4 p.m.,
8 p.m.–midnight,
Sat 8 p.m.–midnight
A rather elegant bistro next to La Pedrera that specializes in fish dishes. $$

La Singular
Metro: Fontana
C/Francesc Giner 50
Tel. 93 237 50 98
Tues–Sun 1–4 p.m.,
9 p.m.–1 a.m.
Run by women, a congenial and inexpensive place for good salads and *tapas*. $

Tábata
Metro: Diagonal
C/Torrent de l'Olla 27
Tel. 93 237 84 96
Mon–Sat 1–4 p.m.,
9 p.m.–midnight
Closed Mon night and Sat midday.
Tasty meat and fish dishes cooked on hot stones known as *tabas*. $$

Tragaluz
Metro: Diagonal
Passatge de la Concepció 5
Tel. 93 487 01 96
Open daily 1.30–4 p.m.,
8.30 p.m.–midnight
(1 a.m. Thurs–Sat)
Superb Mediterranean cuisine in stylish surroundings. $$–$$$

AROUND BARCELONA

Gaig
Metro: Horta
C/Jorge Manrique
Tel. 93 428 03 01
Mon–Sat 1.30–4 p.m.,
8.30 p.m.–midnight,
Sun 1.30–4 p.m.
First-rate traditional Catalan cooking and impressive wine list. $$$

Neichel
Metro: Maria Cristina
C/Beltrán I Rózpide 16 bis
Tel. 93 203 84 08
Mon–Fri 1.30–3.30 p.m.,
Mon–Sat 8.30–11.30 p.m.
Inventive Mediterranean cuisine with a French accent. This is undoubtedly one of Barcelona's most fulfilling ways of off-loading bucketloads of pesetas. $$$

La Venta
FGC train Tibidabo,
then Tramvia Blau
Plaça Doctor Andreu
Tel. 93 212 64 55
Mon–Sat 1.30–3. 15 p.m.,
9–11. 15 p.m.
Next to the Tibidabo funicular, this is probably the best chance to eat well before you get caught up in the snack-food world of the mountain-top funfair. $$–$$$

Entertainment

From opera on La Rambla to rave in the Raval, Barcelona's entertainment scene covers all tastes and types. The best way to find out what's on is to consult the weekly *Guía del Ocio*, the monthly *Informatiu Musical* leaflet or the English-language listings magazine *Barcelona Metropolitan*, which can be picked up at tourist offices. You'll also find a useful local arts and events section in the Friday edition of the national daily *El Pais* and the Barcelona-based *La Vanguardia*.

MAJOR ARTS VENUES

Gran Teatre del Liceu
- Metro: Liceu
- La Rambla 51
- Tel. 93 485 99 00
- Guided tours 9.30 a.m.–11 a.m. daily.

Barcelona's grand 19th-century opera house burnt down in 1994 and has only recently re-opened. It has been transformed into a cutting-edge, high-tech venue, though the auditorium itself has been kept in the original style. You can count on lavish opera productions and big-name singers.

L'Auditori
- Metro: Marina
- Lepant 150
- Tel. 93 247 93 00

Home to the Barcelona Symphony Orchestra and Catalunya National Orchestra, this huge new theatre house is blessed with superb acoustics. Concerts often combine mainstream classical music with works by modern Catalan composers.

Mercat de les Flors
- Metro: Espanya
- Plaça Margarida Xirgu, C/Lleida 59
- Tel. 93 426 18 75

This former flower market was turned into a three-hall venue for music, dance and theatre, including top-flight English-language productions. It's intended as the centrepiece of the new Ciutat del Teatre (City of Theatre), which will also incorporate the Teatre Lliure and the Institut del Teatre.

Palau de la Música Catalana
- Metro: Urquinaona
- C/Sant Francesc de Paula 2
- Tel. 93 295 72 00

Entertainment

Domènech i Montaner's magnificent Modernista theatre provides an unforgettable setting for orchestral classical music and performances of choral music by the Orfeó Catalá choir.

Palau Sant Jordi
- Bus 50
- Passeig Olímpic 57
- Tel. 93 426 20 89

Large-scale concerts of everything from classics to pop in a breathtaking dome-like hall on Montjuïc designed for the 1992 Olympics.

Teatre Lliure
- Metro: Fontana
- C/Montseny 47
- Tel. 93 218 92 51

The bedrock of Catalan theatre, so really only for those keen on engaging with the language. Due to move to the Ciutat del Teatre at the Mercat de les Flors in the near future.

Teatre Nacional de Catalunya
- Metro: Glòries
- Plaça de les Arts 1
- Tel. 900 12 11 33

Vast new theatre putting on drama and dance productions from Catalonia, Spain and the rest of Europe.

BARS AND LIVE MUSIC CLUBS

Almirall
- Metro: Universitat
- C/Joaquín Costa 33
- Tel. 93 412 15 35

This bar has been serving the Raval crowd since the 1860s. Laid-back atmosphere, Modernista décor.

Antilla Cosmopolita
- Metro: Hospital Clinic
- C/Aragó 141
- Tel. 93 451 21 51

Salsa to your heart's content to the strains of first-rate Latin and Caribbean bands.

BOOKING YOUR SEAT

Tickets can be purchased by calling theatres direct, or by using the Tele-entrada service at all branches of the bank Caixa Catalunya. At the Plaça de Catalunya Tourist Office, there is a Tele-entrada outlet where tickets can be bought for half price within three hours of the performance. They also have a phoneline service on 902 10 12 12, and you can reserve on-line at www.telentrada.com. You might also want to try another of Barcelona's saving's bank institutions, Servi-Caixa, which sells tickets over the phone, tel. 902 33 22 11.

Entertainment

L'Ascensor
- Metro: Jaume I
- C/Bellafila 3
- Tel. 93 318 53 47

The entrance is an old elevator (*ascensor*), which gives access to a popular central bar.

La Boîte
- Bus 6,7,15, 27, 32, 33, 34, 67, 68, N12
- Avda Diagonal 477
- Tel. 93 419 59 50
- Information 93 319 17 89

Mainly jazz and blues at this hip basement club in the Eixample. Disco till 5.30 a.m. after the live show.

Bikini
- Metro: Les Corts
- C/Deu I Mata 105
- Tel. 93 322 08 00
- Information 93 322 00 05

Stalwart of the Barcelona music scene for many years, now in a new building. Eclectic bands ranging from Latin American to swing.

Cafè de l'Opera
- Metro: Liceu
- La Rambla 74
- Tel. 93 317 75 85

Barcelona's grandest of grand cafés, with superb turn-of-the-century interior and great location on La Rambla.

Café del Sol
- Metro: Fontana
- Plaça del Sol 16
- Tel. 93 415 56 63

Pleasant, split-level Gràcia bar with tables out on the square for al fresco refreshments.

Club Apolo
- Metro: Paral.lel
- C/Nou de la Rambla 113
- Tel. 93 441 40 01

Superb world music venue with regular acts from Africa, Latin America and the Caribbean.

El Tablao de Carmen
- Metro: Plaça d'Espanya
- C/Arcs 9, Poble Espanyol
- Tel. 93 325 68 95

A great place to enjoy the passion and drama of a quintessential Spanish experience: flamenco.

La Filharmònica
- Metro: Hospital Clinic
- C/Mallorca 204
- Tel. 93 451 11 53

For an enjoyable culture clash, take in jazz, country-blues and a dash of Latin at an English-style pub— serving roast beef for Sunday lunch.

Garatge Club
- Metro: Llacuna
- C/Pallars 195
- Tel. 93 309 14 38

Entertainment

A dazzling hall full of flowers in the Palau de la Música Catalana, Domènech i Montaner's Modernista theatre.

Higher decibel per ear-drum ratio than anywhere else in town at this club dedicated to punk, rock and indie bands.

Harlem Jazz Club
Metro: Jaume I
C/Comtessa de Sobradiel 8
Tel. 93 310 07 55
Fine jazz and Latin in the heart of the medieval old town. Closed Monday.

Jamboree
Metro: Liceu
Plaça Reial 17
Tel. 93 301 75 64

Perennially popular jazz, funk and blues venue, with late-night club after the bands have finished.

La Gran Bodega
Metro: Universitat/Passeig de Gràcia
C/València 193
Tel. 93 453 10 53
A traditional wine bar serving excellent tapas to chase down the wine.

London Bar
Metro: Liceu
C/Nou de la Rambla 34
Tel. 93 318 52 61

Entertainment

Famous late-night pub just off La Rambla, which has counted Picasso and Miró among its regulars.

Luz de Gas
- Bus 6, 7, 15, 27, 30, 32, 33, 34, 58, N8
- C/Muntaner 246
- Tel. 93 209 77 11

With a delightful old theatre providing the stylish backdrop, join a trendy crowd to hear soul, funk, blues, trad and modern jazz.

Marsella
- Metro: Liceu
- C/Sant Pau 65
- Tel. 93 442 72 63

A marvellous relic from the raunchy heyday of the Barrio Chino. Specializes in *absenta* (absinthe), so you can test out Oscar Wilde's dictum that absinthe makes the heart grow fonder.

Mirablau
- FGC train Tibidabo, then Tramvia Blau
- Plaça Doctor Andreu
- Tel. 93 418 58 79

A good stop-off on the way up to Tibidabo, with stunning views.

Nick Havanna
- Metro: Diagonal
- C/Rosselló 208
- Tel. 93 215 65 91

Ultra-trendy, design-conscious 80s bar that gives a snapshot of Barcelona in one of its periodic fits of stylistic excess.

Los Tarantos
- Metro: Liceu
- Plaça Reial 17
- Tel. 616 50 34 97

A good place for flamenco, salsa, Latin and anything else with a Spanish flavour.

NIGHTCLUBS

Barcelona is a late-night city—its clubs don't get going before 1 a.m., and most are still in full party mode at 5 or 6 a.m. Drinks range from inexpensive to pricey, but bear in mind that if you are charged an entrance fee, it will entitle you to one free drink. Dress should be smart-casual.

Galaxy
- Metro: Jaume I
- C/Princesa 53
- Tel. 93 310 10 20

Dark, intimate club, with DJs from London and Barcelona playing pulsating house music. Saturdays only.

Karma
- Metro: Liceu
- Plaça Reial 10
- Tel. 93 302 56 80

Entertainment

Foreign tourists and Barcelona students cram into a basement for mainly rock and pop music.

KGB
- Metro: Joanic
- C/Alegre de Dalt 55
- Tel. 93 210 59 06

Cool crowd and hardcore house scene that starts to crank up the pace when others might be thinking of calling it a night.

Luz de Luna
- Metro: Jaume I/Barceloneta
- C/Comerç 21
- Tel. 93 310 75 42

Salsa, tango and other Latin music, plus the most over-decorated dance floor in town.

Moog
- Metro: Liceu/Drassanes
- C/Arc del Teatre 3
- Tel. 93 301 72 82/
- Information 93 319 17 89

One of the city's hottest spots: 1970s retro disco upstairs, and a powerhouse techno dancefloor below.

Nitsa Club
- Metro: Paral.lel
- C/Nou de la Rambla 113
- Tel. 93 441 40 01

Lively club open till 6 a.m. at weekends, when the pace is never less than hi-energy.

Otto Zutz
- FGC train Gràcia
- C/Lincoln 15
- Tel. 93 238 07 22

Unrivalled as a fashionable nightspot, its three floors fill up with Barcelona's sleekest and chicest clubbers.

Torres de Avila
- Metro: Espanya
- Poble Espanyol, Avda Marquès de Comillas
- Tel. 93 424 93 09

Located in the mock 12th-century gatehouse of the Poble Espanyol, and usually open only at weekends, the club has seven bars on various levels linked by hanging steel staircases and a glass capsule elevator. The décor is postmodern; the summer terrace offers panoramas of the city. Not so much a nightclub as an assault on the senses.

La Paloma
- Metro: Sant Antoni
- Tigre 27
- Tel. 93 301 68 97

Beautiful old style music hall (one of only three of its kind left in Europe), featuring a live Latino orchestra à la Mambo Kings for the over-30s set and top DJs in their ultra-trendy Thurs–Sat late sessions.

The Hard Facts

Airport
El Prat de Llobregat lies 12 km (7.5 miles) southwest of the city. Terminal A deals with arrivals from outside the EU, as well as flights by non-Spanish airlines. Terminal B handles flights by Spanish airlines and EU arrivals. Terminal C is mainly for the Barcelona-Madrid shuttle. Terminals A and B provide foreign exchange and ATM machine services, tourist information offices, newspaper stands, bars, restaurants and duty-free shops.

From outside the terminals you can catch the Aerobus service, leaving every 15 minutes from 5.30 a.m. to 11 p.m. (6 a.m.–10.45 p.m weekends) for Plaça de Catalunya in central Barcelona. The journey takes about 30–40 minutes. There's also a train service. This has the merit of being both slightly cheaper and quicker into the centre, but is less frequent and requires a short walk from the terminals, across a bridge with escalators and moving walkway. Taxis cost anything from 5 to 7 times the price of the train. Taxi ranks can be found immediately outside the terminals.

For general airport information, dial 93 298 38 38.

Climate
The city enjoys a fine, Mediterranean climate. Late spring, early summer and autumn can be marvellously warm and fresh, though there's always the chance of seasonal downpours. July and August are usually very hot and humid, with temperatures reaching up to 37°C—you'll probably find yourself searching for a spot that catches a sea breeze. Winters are often clear and bright, though can be very cold, a reminder of Barcelona's proximity to the Pyrenees.

For information on the weather, tel. 906 36 53 65.

Customs
EU regulations apply. Those travelling from other countries within the EU can import 300 cigarettes, 1.5 litre spirits and 3 litres wine, duty-paid. If entering Spain from a country outside the EU, you can import 200 cigarettes, one litre of spirits, and 5 litres of wine, bought duty-free.

Disabled
While access for disabled travellers to public transport, museums and galleries isn't particularly easy in Barcelona, things are gradually improving—the

The Hard Facts

new Museu d'Art Contemporani de Barcelona, for example, was built with the needs of the disabled in mind. The city's buses, the airport bus and many of its taxis are also equipped to take passengers in wheelchairs. The metro system, however, continues to pose much greater challenges.

For information on facilities at a given museum or restaurant, call the Institut Municipal de Persones amb Disminiució, tel. 93 413 27 75. For transport information for the disabled, tel. 93 486 07 52.

Driving

There's little need to drive around the city—much of the old town is pedestrianized, parking is difficult, and there's an excellent public transport system. If you decide to take a car into the centre, it's probably a good idea to use a car park rather than risk leaving it on the street. Those run by a company called SMASSA can be found at Plaça dels Ángels, near the MACBA gallery, and Moll de la Fusta, by the port; the other main company is SABA, with car parks at Plaça de Catalunya, Plaça Seu and Plaça Urquinaona. Alternatively, Metro-Park is a park-and-ride facility at Plaça de les Glòries, where you can leave your car and hop onto a metro into town, with a one-day metro ticket included in the price of the parking.

A car is useful if you plan to do a lot of touring beyond Barcelona. Note that the speed limit in town is 60 kph (37 mph), while on other roads it's usually 90 kph (56 mph) and on motorways 120 kph (75 mph). Those caught speeding will face on-the-spot fines.

If you bring your own car, be sure to carry your driving licence, car registration document, valid insurance certificate (check that your insurance covers driving in Spain before you leave) and two warning triangles in case of a breakdown.

Catalonia's main automobile club is the Reial Automòbil Club de Catalunya (RACC). For 24-hour breakdown assistance, tel. 902 10 61 06; for information 902 30 73 07. Find out from your own automobile club before you leave whether it is affiliated to the RACC, and if so what services you are entitled to use.

A simpler option might be to hire a car when you are in Barcelona. All the big car hire firms have offices at the airport and in town. It's worth shopping around as well as trying local firms, who often have good deals on offer. You will need to show a valid driving

The Hard Facts

licence, be over 21 (in most cases—and with some firms over 25), and have a credit card for the deposit.

At petrol stations (*gasoliners*), you will have a choice of lead-free petrol (*sense plom* in Catalan, *sin plomo* in Spanish), regular (*super*) and diesel (*gasoil*).

Emergencies
Ambulance: tel. 93 300 20 20
Fire brigade: tel. 080
Police: tel. 092
The Turisme-Atenció police station of the *Guàrdia Urbana* (city police) at La Rambla 43, tel. 93 344 13 00, is designed for tourists who need to report a crime. Officers speak English and French. The station is open 24 hours.

For urgent medical attention head for a hospital casualty department (*Urgències*). The following are centrally located:
Centre d'Urgències
Perecamps
Avda Drassanes 13–15
Tel. 93 441 06 00

Hospital Clinic
C/Villarroel 170
Tel. 93 227 54 00

Dental emergencies:
Centre Odontològic de Barcelona
C/Calàbria 251, baixos
Tel. 93 439 45 00

24-hour pharmacies include:
Farmàcia Clapés
La Rambla 98
Tel. 93 301 28 43

Farmàcia Cervera
C/Muntaner 254
Tel. 93 200 29 57.

Entry Formalities
Most visitors only require a valid passport—and just an identity card for members of the EU. No visa is needed for North American, Australian and New Zealand citizens for stays of up to 3 months. South African citizens not resident in the EU will require a visa, however.

Health
EU nationals are entitled to free medical care, but should obtain an E111 form before leaving home. Non-EU citizens should ascertain whether their country has reciprocal arrangements with Spain. If not, it would be wise to take out health insurance before the journey.

Language
In addition to Catalan, most Barceloneses speak Spanish (*castellano*—Castilian—as it is known there). Catalan is not a dialect of Spanish, rather it's a separate Romance language derived from Latin and with close affinities to Provençal, a

The Hard Facts

language of southern France. At larger hotels, shops and restaurants staff will probably speak some English and French. Otherwise, have a go at some of these basic phrases in Catalan.

Hello	*Hola!*
Good day	*Bon dia*
Goodbye	*Adéu*
Do you speak English?	*Parla anglès?*
Yes/No	*Sí/No*
Thank you	*Gràcies*
Where is…?	*On és…?*
How much is it?	*Quant és?*
Open/closed	*Obert/tancat*

Lost and Found

If you lose something on public transport or around town, contact the city's lost-and-found office:

Servei de Troballes
Ajuntament (Town Hall)
C/Ciutat 9
Tel. 93 402 31 61
Mon–Fri 9 a.m.–2 p.m.

For items lost in taxis, try the Institut Metropolità del Taxi, tel. 93 223 40 12.

For anything lost at the airport, call the main information desk on 93 298 38 38.

Money Matters

Currency. Until January 2002, when Euro coins and banknotes will be issued, the unit of currency is the *peseta* (abbreviated to *pta*, or *pte* in Catalan). Coins: 1, 5, 10, 25, 50, 100, 200 and 500 ptas. Notes: 1,000, 2,000, 5,000 and 10,000 ptas. 1 Euro = 166 ptas.

Banks generally open Mon–Fri from 8.30 a.m.–2 p.m. Outside the summer months they are also open Sat 8.30 a.m.–1 p.m. Bank offices at the airport (in Terminal A and B) and the Barcelona-Sants railway station keep longer hours and are also open at weekends. Exchange bureaux (*cambio* or *canvi*) can be found around town and stay open late, but the rates tend not to be as good. There's an American Express office at La Rambla 74.

Cash Cards. You can draw cash with your ordinary cash card, if it carries the Visa or MasterCard symbol, at most ATM cash machines using your regular PIN code number. Keep in mind that many in the old city now close after 11 p.m

Credit Cards are widely accepted in hotels, restaurants and shops, as are *Traveller's cheques*—don't forget that you need your passport to cash them.

Post Office

In general they open Mon–Fri 8.30 a.m.–2 or 2.30 p.m. The main post office at Plaça d'Antoni López near Port Vell keeps longer hours, opening Mon–Sat 8.30 a.m.–9.30 p.m. for sale of stamps, and with fax and *poste restante* facilities as well. Stamps can also be bought at most *estancos* (tobacconist shops).

Public Holidays
Be prepared to find Barcelona's banks, shops and many of its restaurants, galleries and museums closed on the following public holidays:

Jan 1	New Year's Day
Jan 6	Epiphany
May 1	May Day
June 24	St John the Baptist
Aug 15	Assumption
Sept 11	Catalan National Day
Sept 24	Our Lady of Mercy
Oct 12	Spanish National Day
Nov 1	All Saints' Day
Dec 6	Constitution Day
Dec 8	Immaculate Conception
Dec 25	Christmas Day
Dec 26	Boxing Day

Movable:
March/April Good Friday *(Divendres Sant)*, Easter Monday *(Pasqua Florida)*
May/June Whit Monday *(Pasqua Granada)*

Public Transport
Barcelona has a first-rate public transport network of Ferrocarrils de la Generalitat de Catalunya (FGC) trains, RENFE state trains, metro trains and buses, the latter two being run by the city transport authority (TMB). The metro and FGC operate from about 5 a.m.–11 p.m. during the week, Fri and Sat 5 a.m.–2 a.m., and Sun 6 a.m.–midnight. Buses run from around 6 a.m.–11 p.m. daily, with a night bus service on several routes, picked up from Plaça de Catalunya.
Information:
  TMB   tel. 93 318 70 74
  FGC   tel. 93 205 15 15
  RENFE tel. 93 490 02 02
Note that if you intend to take a train down the coast, you must book your seat in advance.

There's the same flat fare for a single journey on metro, FGC trains and bus, 160 ptas*. There is a variety of options for multi-trip tickets, all giving significant reductions. The Targeta T-1 is a carnet of ten tickets costing 885 ptas, valid on metro, FGC trains, inner-city RENFE trains and buses and able to be shared by two or more people. The Targeta T-50/30 costs 3,700 ptas and allows 50 trips within 30 days. The Targeta T-Mes offers one month's unlimited travel across the network. It's for one person only, costs 5,825 ptas and you need to have a passport-sized photo with you for the ID card.

---

*Prices as of March 2001

And then there are the travelcards. A one-day full-network Targeta T-Dia is 670 ptas; the Targeta 3 Dies gives three days of travel for 1,700 ptas and the Targeta 5 Dies lasts 5 days for 2,600 ptas.

Safety
Barcelona is a fairly safe city for travellers, pickpocketing and bag-snatching in the crowded tourist areas such as La Rambla and the Barri Gòtic is on the rise. It's always sensible to carry out a few basic safety measures. Only carry the money you will need for the day along with a credit card and ATM card. Be careful where you place valuables, wallets, cameras etc and keep a firm grip on handbags and shoulder bags in crowded places, cafes and restaurants. If possible, leave airline tickets, traveller's cheques and extra cash in your hotel safe.

Taxis
The city's black-and-yellow taxis are a reasonable option, especially for two or three people travelling together. They cost more outside normal working hours and a supplement will be added for pieces of luggage and trips to the airport.

Taxi ranks can be found throughout Barcelona at most of the big squares and railway stations, and taxis can also be hailed in the street if they have their green roof-light on. They should also have a sign in the windscreen saying *lliure/libre*, "free".

For general information tel. 010. Reputable firms include:
Barnataxis
tel. 93 357 77 55;
Taxi Ràdio Móvil
tel. 93 358 11 11.

Telephone
The international code for Spain is 34; Barcelona numbers have nine digits, all starting with 93.

To make an international call dial 00, the country code (US and Canada 1, UK 44), area code and local number. You can make overseas calls from public pay phones, or one of the many *locutorios* (call centres) that are dotted around the old city. They are both cheaper than using the phone in your hotel room. Pay phones take coins and phonecards, which can be purchased at post offices and newsstands at 1,000 ptas and 2,000 ptas. Off-peak rates apply on weekdays from 8 p.m.–8 a.m. and all day at weekends.

Directory Enquiries:
  Domestic: 1003
  International: 025

The Hard Facts

Time
From the last Sunday in March to the last Sunday in October, Barcelona follows GMT + 2. In winter, the clocks go back an hour and it becomes GMT + 1. This doesn't affect the time difference with Britain and the US, however, as they change hours at the same moment. Britain is always one hour behind, and New York 6 hours behind.

Tipping
Service will normally be included in restaurant bills, so it's not necessary to leave a tip—but if they are satisfied with the service, locals will tend to leave up to about 5% of the bill. It's also customary to give a 5% tip to taxi drivers, leave the small change in bars and cafés, and tip a small amount to hotel porters and toilet attendants.

Toilets
You won't find public toilets in plentiful supply in Barcelona (and when you come across one it probably won't have any paper, so be prepared). Luckily, bar and café owners are usually pretty relaxed about letting you use the facilities even if you're not a customer. Alternatively, make sure you take advantage of the ones in museums, galleries and restaurants while you're there, as these are often the most spick and span.

Tourist Information Offices
The main tourist office of the Turisme de Barcelona is situated beneath Plaça de Catalunya, open daily 9 a.m.–9 p.m., tel. 906 30 12 82. It's good for maps, city information, souvenirs and does foreign exchange as well. There's also a branch at the Barcelona-Sants railway station, open daily in summer 8 a.m.–8 p.m., but with slightly restricted hours in winter.

The Catalan government also runs offices providing tourist information on the region. Head office:
  Palau Robert building
  Passeig de Gràcia 107
  Tel. 93 238 40 00
  Mon–Sat 10 a.m.–7 p.m.,
  Sun 10 a.m.–2 p.m.
They also have offices at the airport in both Terminal A and Terminal B.

For up-to-date information on sites, museums and so on, call the City Hall Information Service, tel. 010.

Voltage
Electric current is 220-volt 50-cycle AC, and sockets are for plugs with two round pins. British and American equipment will require an adaptor.

Index

Airport 72
Ajuntament de Barcelona 22
Alt Penedès 55
Anella Olímpica 37
Antic Hospital de la Santa Creu 29–30
Aquàrium de Barcelona 33
Auditori 66
Banks 75
Barcelona Card 38
Barceloneta 34
Bars 67–70
Bodegues Torres 56
Caelum 17
Call 23
Casa Amatller 43
– Battló 43
– Bruno Quadras 15
– de l'Ardiaca 19
– Lleó Morera 43
– Museu Gaudí 47
Castell de Montjuïc 35
Catedral La Seu 17–19
Caves Cordoníu 56
Centre de Cultura Contemporánia de Barcelona (CCCB) 29
Centre de Modernisme 43
Climate 72
Clubs 67–71

Col.lecció Thyssen-Bornemisza 50
Colònia Güell 50
Currency 75
Customs 72
Disabled 72–73
Driving 73–74
El Corte Inglés 41
El Triangle 41
Emergencies 74
Entry formalities 74
Església de la Mercè 25
Espai Gaudi 44
Estadi Olímpic 36
Figueres 53
Font de Canaletes 14
Font Màgica 38
Fundació Antoni Tàpies 43
Fundació Joan Miró 35–36
Girona 51
Gràcia 46
Gran Teatre del Liceu 66
Health 74
Hospital Santa Creu i Sant Pau 46
IMAX 33
L'Illa shopping mall 28
La Mercè 23–25
La Pedrera 43–44
La Ribera 25

Language 74–75
Lost and Found 75
Manzana de la Discòrdia 42–43
Mercat de la Boqueria 15
– de los Flors 66
Monestir de Pedralbes 49–50
Money 75
Montserrat 53–55
Monument a Colom 16
Museu
– d'Arqueologia 36–37
– d'Art Contemporani de Barcelona (MACBA) 29
– d'Art Modern de Catalunya 27
– de les Arts Decoratives 48
– Barbier-Mueller d'Art Precolombí 26
– de Cera 16
– de Ceràmica 48
– Diocesà 9–20
– de l'Eròtica 16
– Etnològic 36
– del FC Barcelona 47–48
– Frederic Marès 20
– de Geologia 27

Index

Museu d'Història de Catalunya 33–34
– d'Història de la Ciutat 21
– Marítim 30
– Militar 35
– Nacional Art de Catalunya 37–38
– Picasso 25–26
– Tèxtil i d'Indumentària 26
– de Zoologia 27
Palau de la Generalitat 22
– Güell 30
– de la Música Catalana 66–67
– Reial 21
– Sant Jordi 36, 67
– de la Virreina 15
Parc de la Ciutadella 26–27
– Güell 46–47
Passeig de Gràcia 41
Pavelló Mies van der Rohe 38–39
Pedralbes Centre 28
Pis de la Pedrera 44
Plaça de Catalunya 41
– Duc de Médiniceli 25
– Reial 16
Poble Espanyol 39
Port Aventura 57

Port Olímpic 34
Port Vell 33
Public transport 76–77
Rambla 14–15
Safety 77
Sagrada Família 44–46
Sant Pau del Camp 30
Sant Sadurní d'Anoia 56
Santa Maria del Mar 26
Santa Maria del Pi 17
Sants Just i Pastor 23
Sardana 18
Shopping 28
Sitges 56
Tarragona 56–57
Taxis 77
Teatre Lliure 67
– Nacional de Catalunya 67
– Poliorama 14
Telefònica tower 36
Telephone 77
Temple d'Augustus 22
Tibidabo 49
Torre de Collserola 49
Vila Olímpica 34
Vilafranca del Penedès 55–56
Vinçon 42

GENERAL EDITOR:
Barbara Ender-Jones
RESEARCH:
Suzanne Wales
LAYOUT:
Luc Malherbe
PHOTO CREDITS:
Ingrid Morató back cover, pp. 1, 4, 9, 19, 31, 32, 36, 69;
Hémisphères/Borredon front cover;
Hémisphères/Gardel pp. 2, 7, 10, 24, 40, 48;
Hémisphères/Rieger p. 15;
Hémisphères/Frilet p. 28;
Hémisphères/Felix pp. 39, 44;
Reporters/Gabriel p. 62
MAPS:
Kartographie Huber;
Elsner & Schichor;
JPM Publications

Copyright © 2001
by JPM Publications S.A.
12, avenue William-Fraisse,
1006 Lausanne, Switzerland
information@jpmguides.com
http://www.jpmguides.com/

All rights reserved. No part of this book may be reproduced or transmitted in any form or by any means, electronic or mechanical, including photocopying, recording or by any information storage and retrieval system without permission in writing from the publisher.
Every care has been taken to verify the information in the guide, but neither the publisher nor his client can accept responsibility for any errors that may have occurred. If you spot an inaccuracy or a serious omission, please let us know.

Printed in Switzerland
Weber/Bienne (CTP) — 01/01/05